# Breaking Away from the Algebra and Geometry Book

*Original and Traditional Lessons for Grades K–8*

Patricia Baggett
Andrzej Ehrenfeucht

scarecrow
education

The Scarecrow Press, Inc.
A Scarecrow Education Book
Lanham, Maryland, and London
2001

SCARECROW PRESS, INC.
A Scarecrow Education Book

Published in the United States of America
by Scarecrow Press, Inc.
4720 Boston Way, Lanham, Maryland 20706
www.scarecroweducation.com

4 Pleydell Gardens, Folkestone
Kent CT20 2DN, England

British Library Cataloguing in Publication Information Available

**Library of Congress Cataloging-in-Publication Data**

Baggett, Patricia.
    Breaking away from the algebra and geometry book : original and
traditional lessons for grades K–8 / Patricia Baggett, Andrzej Ehrenfeucht.
        p.   cm. — (A Scarecrow education book)
    ISBN 0-8108-4048-0 (pbk. : alk. paper)
    1. Algebra—Study and teaching (Elementary)  2. Algebra—Study and
teaching (Middle school)  3. Geometry—Study and teaching (Elementary)
4. Geometry—Study and teaching (Middle school)  I. Ehrenfeucht, Andrzej.
II. Title.
QA159 .B337  2001
372.7—dc21                                              2001034473

♾™ The paper used in this publication meets the minimum requirements of
American National Standard for Information Sciences—Permanence of
Paper for Printed Library Materials, ANSI/NISO Z39.48-1992.
Manufactured in the United States of America.

*In memory of Aniela Ehrenfeucht (1905–1999)*
*and Caroline Peterson Merkle (1899–1989).*

# CONTENTS

# PREFACE

Young children like arithmetic. When asked about their favorite school subjects, most first and second graders list math among them. Even students who find learning difficult are usually interested in numbers and often spend a large amount of time mastering arithmetic. But by the end of middle school the situation is different. Many students dislike mathematics, and some have developed a fear of it. One subject that is responsible for this change of attitude is middle-school algebra. Many students find it difficult, boring, and useless.

This book introduces algebra differently. It provides 62 classroom-tested lessons for elementary and middle grades in which algebra is introduced early and merged with other mathematical techniques. Many lessons are geometrical and contain a substantial hands-on component, and some can be used as early as kindergarten, first, and second grade. Some of the lessons are original, but many others are traditional—invented hundreds or thousands of years ago and passed down from generation to generation.

# ACKNOWLEDGMENTS

This book is the third in the Breaking Away series, and a number of people and organizations have helped to bring it to fruition. Karin Matray, director of professional development for the Las Cruces (New Mexico) public schools, has given a huge amount of unwavering support and encouragement to us for six years, since we first began working in her district. About four years ago we discussed with her concerns about the math curricula in her district, and she and others in the district identified algebra and geometry as topics that needed more emphasis. So together we approached the Exxon (now ExxonMobil) Education Foundation for funding to develop a new university algebra and geometry course for prospective and practicing K–8 teachers. We especially thank Robert Witte and Jean Moon of ExxonMobil for sponsoring the course for three semesters. This book contains the bulk of the materials developed for the course.

The Las Cruces public school teachers who enrolled in the course also deserve special thanks. They studied the lessons in this book, and then tried with their students those that they judged to be suitable, reporting back to us on their successes and limitations. This feedback helped us to improve the lesson plans. They also allowed Professor Baggett to try lessons in their classrooms regularly. Teachers of early elementary children often tried advanced lessons with young learners, with a high success rate. "Never underestimate what a child can do!" became the motto in the classes. We include in the book teachers' reports of how two lessons were presented to young children. We were especially happy to see children in kindergarten and first grade measuring in centimeters and millimeters, using compasses to draw circles and arcs, and using protractors to measure angles.

New Mexico State University undergraduates who were prospective teachers enrolled in the same university math course with the public school teachers. (We call these joint courses partnership courses.) The undergraduates served as apprentices to their mentoring teachers, helping them to teach the lessons to children. We thank them for their participation and enthusiasm, and for the risks they were willing to take. They learned to adapt lessons to different ages and grades, and they expressed surprise and delight at what children could do.

The New Mexico State University College of Education has also supported this work. We thank Professor Patrick Scott for using New Mexico Collaborative for Excellence in Teacher Preparation (NMCETP) funding to sponsor teaching assistants for the algebra and geometry course, and also for helping to recruit undergraduates to take the course.

We thank Vanessa Galarza, Chris Moreno, and John Pierce for helping us develop the website http://math.nmsu.edu/breakingaway/. It continues to evolve, contains a number of mathematics units, and can be used as a companion to this book.

We also thank Chris Moreno and Laura Woodward for preparing illustrations for the book.

# INTRODUCTION

From its humble beginnings as the art of solving equations, algebra has spread throughout all of mathematics, and to its relatives, statistics, theoretical physics, and computer science. Variables, algebraic expressions, and formulas, as well as the techniques of handling them, are used in all domains of mathematics without a single exception. Thus viewing algebra as just one of many mathematical theories misrepresents its role and importance in modern mathematics.

The point of view expressed in this book is that algebra is a part of all domains of mathematics. The book provides lesson plans that cover many topics: a variety of traditional word problems, arithmetic, two- and three-dimensional geometry based on measurement, and combinatorics, games, and puzzles. We see how in all these domains the use of algebra simplifies and clarifies the solutions.

But mathematics has no "silver bullet." Many problems can also be solved by other methods, and some of them leave no room for algebra.

Calculators are used in many problems. You may need either a simple four-operation calculator, or a scientific one. For more advanced students, scientific calculators are better. For beginners, simpler calculators are easier to master, and they do not distract from the task at hand.

# Arithmetic and Algebra
## Part A:
## Word Problems

## LESSON 1  VARIABLES IN EARLY GRADES

Even in kindergarten, children are asked questions similar to this one: "We have 5 paper plates. How many more do we need in order to have 8?" Problems start when such questions are given in written form. You may see something like this:

$$5 + \underline{\ \ } = 8,$$

or even like this:

$$5 + \square = 8.$$

Both versions are unsatisfactory. Mathematical formulas should be readable. And if we try to read aloud these texts and to explain what the task is, we run into trouble. "Five plus blank space equals eight" and "Five plus a square equals eight" do not make much sense. And instructions such as "Write a number in the empty space to make the equation true" suggest mindless and unnecessary drill.

Here is an example of a better approach. We know two numbers, 5 and 8. The third one is unknown, so let's name it $U$. We know that 5 plus $U$ equals 8. We can write it down as:

$$5 + U = 8.$$

Now we have to find out what $U$ is. Let's first write it differently, as "$U$ plus 5 equals 8":

$$U + 5 = 8.$$

So:

$$U + 4 = 7$$
$$U + 3 = 6$$
$$U + 2 = 5$$
$$U + 1 = 4$$

and finally:

$$U = 3.$$

So now we know that $U$ is 3.

## REMARKS

In this approach everything that is written is also spoken, and $U$ is simply the name of an unknown number we are trying to find.

This approach also allows you to discuss different methods. Here is one that may be a little more difficult for young children:

$$U + 5 = 8.$$

So:

$$U + 5 - 5 = 8 - 5$$
$$U = 8 - 5$$
$$U = 3.$$

## LESSON 2    WRITING EQUATIONS

Problem solving has many aspects. Performing arithmetic operations is only one of them. The skill of writing equations is probably more important, and it can be taught much earlier than it is done now. Consider the following standard problem.

> Jim has 27 peanuts, and Mary has only 12. How many peanuts should Jim give Mary so that each of them has the same amount?

## A SOLUTION

(1) Choosing a variable.

Let's name the (unknown at present) number of peanuts that Jim should give Mary, $N$. (I like $N$ because it is the first letter of the word number. But if you prefer $P$ for peanuts, it is fine with me.)

(2) Writing an equation.

After Jim gives $N$ peanuts to Mary, he still has

$$27 - N$$

peanuts, and Mary has

$$12 + N$$

peanuts. But these two numbers are now equal, and therefore:

$$27 - N = 12 + N.$$

(3) Solving the equation.

Many methods are available for solving an equation. Here is one based on the principle that for all numbers $A$, $B$, $C$, and $D$, if $A - B = C + D$, then $A - C = B + D$.

We know that:        $27 - N = 12 + N,$

and therefore:        $27 - 12 = N + N,$

so:                         $15 = 2 * N,$

and finally:             $N = 7\frac{1}{2}.$

(4) Checking the solution.

$$27 - 7\frac{1}{2} = 19\frac{1}{2},$$

and:                        $12 + 7\frac{1}{2} = 19\frac{1}{2}.$

(5) Answering the original question.

Jim should give Mary 7½ peanuts. Cutting a peanut in half is silly, so he should give her 7 or 8 peanuts. What do you think?

## REMARK

We have used this unit as a hands-on activity. Two children each grab a handful of peanuts. They must share so that each person has the same number. How would you help them do it?

## LESSON 3   HEADS AND LEGS

Problem solving is high on the list of topics that are recommended by the National Council of Teachers of Mathematics (NCTM). It has brought back into schools many old problems that have amused, or tormented, students for several centuries. Here is one of them.

In a park some children were playing with some dogs. The total number of heads was 7, and the total number of legs was 20. What was the number of tails in the park?

Such problems can be solved in many different ways, for example, by making a table.

| Number of children | 0 | 1 | 2 | 3 | 4 | 5 | 6 | 7 |
|---|---|---|---|---|---|---|---|---|
| Number of dogs (also number of tails!) | 7 | 6 | 5 | 4 | 3 | 2 | 1 | 0 |
| Number of legs | 28 | 26 | 24 | 22 | 20 | 18 | 16 | 14 |

Because the total number of legs was 20, the answer is in the column with 20 legs, which means 3 tails were in the park.

But in mathematics, most of the time we are not just interested in the answer. We want to find a general solution that turns a problem into a routine exercise. Algebra provides techniques for turning challenging problems into routine tasks.

Let

$C$          be the number of children;

$D$          be the number of dogs, and also the number of tails;

$L = 20$     be the number of legs;

$H = 7$      be the number of heads.

We know that   $C + D = H$,

and          $2*C + 4*D = L.$

Thus         $2*C + 2*D = 2*H$

and          $(2*C + 4*D) - (2*C + 2*D) = L - 2*H.$

Therefore    $2*D = L - 2*H.$

And finally  $D = L/2 - H.$

This formula gives the general solution to the problem:

The number of tails is one half of the number of legs minus the number of heads.

## APPROACH FOR A KINDERGARTEN CLASSROOM

Here is what Leslie Jackson, a kindergarten teacher, wrote in her journal after trying this problem in her class:

"The children used 7 circles out of construction paper for heads, 20 brown rectangles for legs. A large green construction paper was used as a background to glue on circles and rectangles so the children would not lose parts.

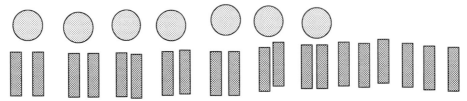

*There were 7 heads and 20 legs in the park.*

We told the children they went for a walk in the park. There were some children playing with dogs. If we counted all the heads in the park we would count 7. So the children glued the seven heads onto the grass (green construction paper). The children then were told there were 20 legs. I asked the children how many legs the people had. The answer was 2. How many legs do dogs have? The answer was 4. I told the children they must use all of the legs. They were allowed to work with each other. Kinders like to have their own work, so they each had a paper, but did a lot of talking. Many of the kinders were able to complete it, others were distracted. Some of the children took the initiative to count and write totals of people and dogs on their paper."

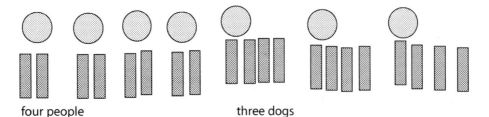

four people                          three dogs

*Kindergartners arranged them to make four children and three dogs.*

How it might be improved:

"The children enjoyed figuring out this activity. Once they did they were really proud of themselves. I would like to continue problem-solving projects like this with the kinders. There is a lot of math involved in this activity for kinders."

My reactions to it:

"This project worked well. I did not use pennies and peanuts [one way that we had solved the problem in the university class] because the kinders would become too distracted with eating the peanuts and counting the pennies. It worked very well with the shapes."

## LESSON 4   FOUR NUMBERS

Can you find four consecutive odd numbers that add up to 80?

### AN ALGEBRAIC SOLUTION

Let's name the first number $n$. Then the second one is $n + 2$, the third is $n + 4$, and the fourth is $n + 6$. Because they add up to 80, we have

$$n + n + 2 + n + 4 + n + 6 = 80.$$

Thus $4*n = 80 - 12 = 68$, and therefore $n = 17$. So the solution is

17, 19, 21, 23.

We can check it mentally; 17 plus 23 is 40, and 19 plus 21 is also 40, so together they add up to 80.

### AN ARITHMETIC SOLUTION

Let's make a "false assumption" that the numbers are

11, 13, 15, 17.

(Or choose any other four consecutive odd numbers.) Their sum is

$$11 + 13 + 15 + 17 = 56.$$

But $80 - 56 = 24$, so the sum is too small. One quarter of the difference is $24/4 = 6$, so let's increase each of the four numbers by this amount, to $11 + 6$, $13 + 6$, $15 + 6$, and $17 + 6$. Now we have the correct answer:

17, 19, 21, 23.

### COMMENT

This method of "false assumption" was already known to ancient Egyptians 4,000 years ago. (See also lessons 5, 6, and 7, "Push-Ups," "Sharing Apples," and "Bottle and Cork.")

### TEACHING THE UNIT IN THIRD GRADE

Here is a third grader's description of how he solved the problem (with spelling preserved), together with the comments of his teacher, Susan Tellez, as written in her journal.

> *Child:* We had to find the odd number between 0 and 100. We said that an odd number is a number that can't be shared equally. We used students in a game to find the odd and even numbers. Then we colored a 100 chart. We practiced adding doubles

like 2 + 2 and 20 + 20; 4 + 4 and 40 + 40. Next we picked any for consecutive odd number we added the front digits to see how colse we could get to 80 we crossed out the numbers that did not equal 80 we crossed rows 51 to 100 and rows 31–50. We used a calculator to find the answer. The four consecutive odd numbers that equal 80 are: 17, 19, 21, 23.

*Ms. Tellez:* You had a *fantastic* understanding of how to get 80. Don't forget to show your mom and dad how you got 80 which no one else could do!! Did you like this problem? Why/why not?

*Child:* I like it becsuze I like Math and working with calculator and I like the problem becuze it is a Math problem.

*Ms. Tellez:* [Child's name] came up to me after he finished his writing. Following are his words used to express his understanding afterwards!

"Mrs. Tellez, I get it!

17        19        21        23

I added the 2 and 2 and that gave me 40.

17        19        21        23

Then I added the 1 and the 1 and that gave me another 20 which gave me 60. If I add the 7 and 3 I get 10 and that's 70. And if I add 9 and 1 I get another 10 which gives me 80!"

This was "fantastic"!

## LESSON 5   PUSH-UPS

Sally did push-ups five days in a row. On each day she did 10 more push-ups than on the previous day. In all, she did 210 push-ups. How many did she do on each day?

Of the several methods of solving this problem, the oldest one (called "false supposition" or "false position") was known to Ahmes (Ahmose, in the Rhind papyrus, an ancient Egyptian text dated in the seventeenth century B.C.E.).

Here are some different methods.

(1) Algebraic

Let's call the unknown number she did on the first day sally. So the number of push-ups was:

| | |
|---|---|
| 1st day | sally |
| 2nd day | sally + 10 |
| 3rd day | sally + 20 |
| 4th day | sally + 30 |
| 5th day | sally + 40 |

So the total was 5*sally (five times sally) plus 100. (You add 1 + 2 + 3 + 4 mentally, saying one, three, six, ten; and multiply it by ten, saying times ten, a hundred.) Therefore we know that

$$210 = 100 + 5*sally.$$

So

$$210 - 100 = 5*sally,$$
$$110 = 5*sally.$$

So

$$110/5 = sally.$$

The answer is sally = 22, and therefore

| | |
|---|---|
| 1st day | 22 |
| 2nd day | 32 |
| 3rd day | 42 |
| 4th day | 52 |
| 5th day | 62 |
| Total | 210 (use a calculator here). |

(2) False supposition

Assume that she started with 10 push-ups (or any other number), and see how many off we are.

| | |
|---|---|
| 1st day | 10 |
| 2nd day | 20 |
| 3rd day | 30 |
| 4th day | 40 |
| 5th day | 50 |
| Total | 150 |

Because 210 − 150 = 60, we are off by 60. But the push-ups happened over five days. So we are off by 60/5 = 12 push-ups per day.

Answer:

| | |
|---|---|
| 1st day | 10 + 12 = 22 |
| 2nd day | 20 + 12 = 32 |
| 3rd day | 30 + 12 = 42 |
| 4th day | 40 + 12 = 52 |
| 5th day | 50 + 12 = 62 |

(3) By subtracting extras using a calculator

Let's divide the push-ups into a basic number that was the same for every day, and extras done each day. Subtract the extras from the total and find how many basic push-ups were done per day.

| | | | |
|---|---|---|---|
| [210][−][10] | [=] | subtract second-day extras; | |
| | [=][=] | subtract third-day extras; | |
| | [=][=][=] | subtract fourth-day extras; | |
| | [=][=][=][=] | subtract fifth-day extras; | |
| [/][5] | [=] | display: 22 | 1st day; |
| [+][10] | [=] | display: 32 | 2nd day; |
| | [=] | display: 42 | 3rd day; |
| | [=] | display: 52 | 4th day; |
| | [=] | display: 62 | 5th day. |

(4) Guess and check

Program for the TI-108 calculator.

[MRC][MRC] [guess][M+] [+][10]

[=][M+] [=][M+] [=][M+] [=][M+] (four times)

[MRC]

If the number on the display is not 210, our guess is incorrect. One way we can correct it is by using the method of false supposition presented earlier.

## LESSON 6   SHARING APPLES

I had some apples in a basket. I gave 1/2 of them to my older sister, 1/6 of them to my younger sister, and 1/4 of them to my twin brother. I ate the last apple. How many apples did I have in my basket?

### AN ALGEBRAIC SOLUTION (USING A TI-108 CALCULATOR)

Name the unknown number of apples in the basket $X$.

How many were given away?   $X/2 + X/6 + X/4$.

How many were left?       $X - X/2 - X/6 - X/4$.

Therefore we know that

$$X - X/2 - X/6 - X/4 = 1.$$

But

$$X - X/2 - X/6 - X/4 = X*(1 - 1/2 - 1/6 - 1/4) = 1.$$

So

$$X = 1/(1 - 1/2 - 1/6 - 1/4).$$

Program (start with a clear calculator).

[1][M+][2][/][M–][6][/][M–][4][/][M–] [MRC][/][=]

The program returns 11.99999, so $X = 12$.

Check the solution mentally: "1/2 of 12 is 6, 1/6 of 12 is 2, and 1/4 of 12 is 3.

6 + 2 + 3  make 11, so 1 apple was left."

### REMARKS

• With some experience the algebraic part of the computation can also be done mentally.

• You can use calculators to compute with common fractions.

• This problem can also be solved by the rule of false position:

"Suppose I guess that I had 24 apples originally. I gave away half, or 12, to my older sister 1/6, or 4, to my younger sister; and 1/4, or 6, to my twin brother. 12 + 4 + 6 = 22, and 24 – 22 = 2, which is twice as many as I should have left. 24 ÷ 2 = 12. Therefore I started with 12."

## LESSON 7   BOTTLE AND CORK

This very old word problem is repeated here mainly for amusement. At the end we show how to solve it using an old method called "false position."

A bottle and a cork cost $1.10. The bottle costs $1 more than the cork. How much does each of them cost?

### ALGEBRAIC SOLUTION

Name the unknown numbers:

$b$   cost of the bottle in dollars;

$c$   cost of the cork in dollars.

Write two equations:

$$b + c = 1.10$$

$$b - c = 1$$

Solve the equations by adding both sides of the preceding two equations:

$$2*b = 2.10$$

$$b = 1.05$$

And therefore

$$c = 0.05.$$

Write the answer:

The bottle costs $1.05, and the cork costs 5 cents.

### OLD ARITHMETIC SOLUTION

Let's assume the bottle costs 90¢, and therefore the cork costs 20¢. But then the difference is 70¢, which is 30¢ less than required. Half of 30¢ is 15¢. So let the cost of the bottle be 90¢ + 15¢ = $1.05, and the cost of the cork be 20¢ − 15¢ = 5¢, and we have the solution.

You may start with other numbers: Let's assume the bottle costs $1, and therefore the cork costs 10¢. But then the difference is 90¢, which is 10¢ less than required. Half of 10¢ is 5¢. So let the cost of the bottle be $1 + 5¢ = $1.05, and the cost of the cork be 10¢ − 5¢ = 5¢, and we have the solution.

Let's assume the bottle costs $1.08, and therefore the cork costs 2¢. But then the difference is  $1.06, which is 6¢ more than required. Half of 6¢ is 3¢. So let the cost of the bottle be $1.08 - 3¢ = $1.05$, and the cost of the cork be $2¢ + 3¢ = 5¢$, and we have the solution.

This process is an example of an old method called "false position." False position meant a false assumption, from the verb, "posit," which means to postulate. In this method you just try to guess the answer, but only once. Then you see how much your guess is off, and you correct it to get the right answer.

How does this method work? We may use algebra to analyze it. We do not know $b$ and $c$, but we only know that $b + c = \$1.10$ and $b - c = \$1$. So we choose any two values $b'$ and $c'$ such that $b' + c' = \$1.10$. These values are our false assumption.

Now we compute $b' - c'$, and $e = (b - c) - (b' - c')$. The value $e$ is the error that we are making. If $e > 0$, the cost of the bottle was underestimated, and if $e < 0$, it was overestimated.

So we take $b = b' + e/2$ and $c = c' - e/2$.

Let's check this solution:

$$b + c = b' + e/2 + c' - e/2 = b' + c' = \$1.10.$$

$$b - c = b' + e/2 - c' + e/2 = b' - c' + e = \$1.$$

## LESSON 8    POOR PEPPERMINT PATTY

In a "Peanuts" cartoon, Patty reads,

> A man has twenty coins consisting of dimes and quarters. If the dimes were quarters and the quarters were dimes, he would have ninety cents more than he has now. How many dimes and quarters does he have?

She thinks for a while, and shouts, "HELP!!!"

Poor Peppermint Patty! She doesn't know algebra!

### TASK

Solve this problem. But, no calculators, no paper and pencil, no manipulatives, . . . only your brain.

(1) The computation is so simple that anyone can do it mentally.

$$25 - 10 = 15$$
$$90/15 = 6$$
$$(20 + 6)/2 = 13 \quad \text{(the number of dimes)}$$
$$13 - 6 = 7 \qquad \text{(the number of quarters)}$$

But how can we plan this computation?

You may think:

A quarter is worth 15 cents more than a dime, and there are six fifteen cents in 90 cents, so he must have 6 more dimes than quarters. But together he has 20 coins. So 6 + 20 is twice the number of dimes.

The number of dimes is 13, and the number of quarters is $13 - 6 = 7$.

Why do we call it algebra? It is the same reasoning that, written in algebraic jargon, looks as follows:

Let $d$ be the number of dimes; let $q$ be the number of quarters.

Then $10^*d + 25^*q$ is the amount of money he has now.

And if dimes were quarters, and quarters were dimes, he would have $25^*d + 10^*q$.

If we subtract the first amount from the second amount, he would have 90 cents.

So:

$$25^*d + 10^*q - (10^*d + 25^*q) = (25 - 10)^*d + (10 - 25)^*q = 15^*(d - q) = 90;$$

Divide both sides by 15:

$$d - q = 90/15 = 6. \qquad (1)$$

We know that he had twenty coins altogether, so

$$d + q = 20. \qquad (2)$$

We add equations (1) and (2) together:

$$2*d = 26$$
$$d = 13;$$
$$q = d - (d - q) = d - 6 = 7.$$

Here is a way to solve the problem using a table:

A quarter is worth 15 cents more than a dime, and there are six 15 cents in 90 cents, so he must have six more dimes than quarters. So he could have:

| Number of dimes | Number of quarters | Number of coins | Money he has | Money he would have | Difference |
|:---:|:---:|:---:|:---:|:---:|:---:|
| 6 | 0 | 6 | $.60 | $1.50 | $ .90 |
| 7 | 1 | 8 | .95 | 1.85 | .90 |
| 8 | 2 | 10 | 1.30 | 2.20 | .90 |
| 9 | 3 | 12 | 1.65 | 2.55 | .90 |
| 10 | 4 | 14 | 2.00 | 2.90 | .90 |
| 11 | 5 | 16 | 2.35 | 3.15 | .90 |
| 12 | 6 | 18 | 2.70 | 3.60 | .90 |
| 13 | 7 | 20 | 3.05 | 3.95 | .90 |

Because he has 20 coins, the last row contains the answer.

(2) Let's solve a more general problem using the TI-30X IIS calculator.

> A man has $X$ coins consisting of dimes and quarters. If the dimes were quarters and the quarters were dimes, he would have $Y$ cents more than he has now. How many dimes and quarters does he have?

We cannot give a numerical answer without knowing the values of $X$ (the number of coins he has) and $Y$ (the extra amount he would have, if his dimes were quarters and his quarters were dimes). But we can prepare a program that provides such answers.

## WRITE A PLAN

| | |
|---|---|
| $Y/15$ = answer1 | (number of dimes – number of quarters) |
| $(X +$ answer1$)/2$ = answer2 | (the number of dimes) |
| answer2 – answer1 = answer3 | (the number of quarters) |

## WRITE A PROGRAM

We use variable $A$ to store answer1.
Enter:

| | | |
|---|---|---|
| $Y/15 \;\rightarrow\; A$ | [=] | |
| $(X +$ Ans$)/2$ | [=] | write down the number of dimes; |
| Ans-A | [=] | write down the number of quarters. |

## LESSON 9    SHEEP: AN OLD PUZZLE

Two farmers, Fred and Violet, were taking their sheep to market. Fred said, "Give me one of your sheep so we will both have the same number." Violet answered, "No! Instead, you better give me one of yours, so I'll have twice as many as you have."

How many sheep did each of them have?

### AN ALGEBRAIC SOLUTION

Name the unknown numbers:

$x$        the number of sheep Fred has

$y$        the number of sheep Violet has

Write two equations:

$$x + 1 = y - 1$$
$$y + 1 = 2*(x - 1)$$

Solve the equations:

$$x + 2 = y$$
$$y = 2*x - 3$$

Thus:

$$x + 2 = 2*x - 3$$

Therefore:

$$5 = x$$
$$7 = y$$

Check the solution mentally.

Write the answer:

The first farmer, Fred, had 5 sheep, and the second, Violet, had 7.

## AN ARITHMETIC SOLUTION

If giving away one sheep makes their number equal, then their difference is 2. So Violet has two more sheep than Fred. If Fred gives one sheep to Violet, the difference increases to 4. But then Violet has twice as many as Fred. So then the numbers are 4 and 8. Thus the original numbers are 5 and 7.

## LESSON 10    CUBES, BALLS, AND NAILS

In a book for teachers we found the following problem nicely illustrated with balance scales:

> Two cubes and two balls balance fourteen nails. One cube and two nails balance two balls and three nails. How many nails are needed to balance one cube?

There are many different ways, including guess and check, to solve this problem. But an algebraic approach removes all challenge by reducing the problem to a routine computation, which will provide a correct answer even in the case when the answer is not a whole number.

Let:

$c$        be the weight of one cube;

$b$        be the weight of one ball; and

$n$        be the weight of one nail.

We know that:

(1)   $2*c + 2*b = 14*n$

(2)     $c + 2*n = 2*b + 3*n$

From equation (2) we know that:

(3)   $c - 2*b = n$

Adding both sides of equations (1) and (3), we have:

(4)   $3*c = 15*n$

Therefore $c = 5*n$, which means that one cube weighs as much as five nails.

## REMARK

This typical use of elementary algebra allows you to compute with "unknown" numbers, represented by identifiers such as $x$, $y$, and $z$, as easily as or even more easily than with numbers represented in any standard notation. Thus elementary algebra can be viewed as an extension of arithmetic techniques and not as a new mathematical topic, and it may be started earlier than is currently done.

## LESSON 11   AGES OF MOTHER AND DAUGHTER: A PUZZLE

In two years I will be three times younger than my mother. Two years ago I was four times younger than my mother. How old am I? How old is my mother?

### SOLUTION

You can solve this problem by trying different numbers until you find the right one. But a better method is provided by algebra.

You do not know the person's age or her mother's age (we are assuming that a daughter is talking), but you can name these unknown numbers $x$ and $y$. Mathematicians usually name unknown numbers $x$ and $y$.

Her age two years ago was $x - 2$. Her mother's age was $y - 2$.

But at that time she was 4 times younger than her mother.

Therefore (mathematicians like to use "therefore"):

$$(x - 2)*4 = y - 2.$$

The parentheses show that first you subtract 2 from $x$, and then you multiply the difference by 4.

The girl's age in 2 years will be $x + 2$, and her mother's age will be $y + 2$. But then she will be three times younger than her mother. Therefore:

$$(x + 2)*3 = y + 2.$$

This formula and the preceding formula are called equations.

But $(x - 2)*4 = x*4 - 8$, and similarly

$$(x + 2)*3 = x*3 + 6.$$

(These are facts of arithmetic. Did you know that for all numbers $a$, $b$, and $c$, $(a - b)*c = a*c - b*c$, and $(a + b)*c = a*c + b*c$?)

Therefore:

$$x*4 - 8 = y - 2$$
$$x*3 + 6 = y + 2$$

But then:

$$x*4 - 8 + 2 = y$$
$$x*3 + 6 - 2 = y$$

Here we used these facts: If $a = b + c$ then $a - c = b$; and if $a = b - c$ then $a + c = b$.

So:

$x*4 - 6 = x*3 + 4$

Why? Because two numbers equal to a third (here the third number is $y$), are equal. Therefore:

$x*4 - x*3 = 4 + 6$

Which facts of arithmetic did we use here?

So:

$x*(4 - 3) = 10$

Therefore:

$x = 10$

The girl is 10 years old.

But we know that $x*4 - 6 = y$, so $y = 10*4 - 6 = 34$.
Her mother is 34 years old.

Check the solution:

Two years ago she was 8 and her mother was 32, $4*8 = 32$, so she was four times younger than her mother.

In two years she will be 12 and her mother will be 36, $3*12 = 36$, so she will be three times younger than her mother.

**LESSON 12  WEDDING DAY**

This poem comes from a book published in 1799 in London by Charles Vyse. Augustus de Morgan, in his *Arithmetical Books from the Invention of Printing to the Present Time* (London: Taylor and Walton, 1847) called Vyse "one of the most celebrated of the illustrious band who used to adorn the shelves of a country schoolmaster at the beginning of this century. . . . The following specimen of the muse of arithmetic should be preserved, as the best known in its day, and the most classical of its kind":

> When first the Marriage-Knot was tied
>   Between my Wife and me,
> My Age did her's as far exceed
>   As three Times three does three;
> But when ten Years, and Half ten Years,
>   We Man and Wife had been,
> Her Age came up as near to mine
>   As eight is to sixteen.
> Now, tell me, I pray,
> What were our Ages on the Wedding Day?

## A SOLUTION

We interpret the wedding day ages to be in the ratio 3 to 1; after 15 years we interpret them to be in the ratio 2 to 1.

On the wedding day:

$$x = \text{his age}$$
$$1/3\ x = \text{her age}$$

After 15 years:

$x + 15$ = his age

$1/2*(x + 15)$ = her age

So:

$1/3*x + 15 = 1/2*(x + 15)$

$2*x + 90 = 3*(x + 15)$  (multiplying by 6)

$2*x + 90 = 3*x + 45$

When married:

$x = 45$

$1/3\ x = 15$

After 15 years:

$x + 15 = 60$

$1/2*(x + 15) = 30$

The husband was 45 and the wife 15 on their wedding day. After 15 years, he was 60 and she was 30.

## LESSON 13   A MOST DREADED WORD PROBLEM

Some word problems strike terror in the hearts of students. This problem is one of them.

> Jack can weed $3/4$ of a garden in $4\frac{1}{2}$ hours. Jill can weed $1/2$ of the same garden in $3\frac{1}{3}$ hours. How long it will take them to weed $1/2$ of the garden working together?

Constants and variables:

| | | |
|---|---|---|
| $a_1 = \frac{3}{4}$ | (of a garden) | amount of work Jack does; |
| $t_1 = 4\frac{1}{2}$ | (hours) | time to do it; |
| $r_1 = a_1/t_1$ | (garden per hour) | the rate of Jack's weeding; |
| | | |
| $a_2 = \frac{1}{2}$ | (of a garden) | amount of work Jill does; |
| $t_2 = 3\frac{1}{3}$ | (hours) | time to do it; |
| $r_2 = a_2/t_2$ | (garden per hour) | the rate of Jill's weeding; |
| | | |
| $A = \frac{1}{2}$ | (of a garden) | work to be done by both; |
| $T$ | (hours) | unknown time to do it; |
| $R = r_1 + r_2$ | (garden per hour) | the rate of their work. |

Equation:

$$A = R*T$$

The total amount of work is the rate times the time.

Solving for $T$:

$$T = A/R = A/(r_1 + r_2) = A/(a_1/t_1 + a_2/t_2).$$

We show three ways to compute the solution.

(1) A paper and pencil solution:

$a_1 = \frac{3}{4}$,      $t_1 = \frac{9}{2}$,      $a_1/t_1 = \frac{6}{36} = \frac{1}{6}$

$a_2 = \frac{1}{2}$,      $t_2 = \frac{10}{3}$      $a_2/t_2 = \frac{3}{20}$

                    sum $= a_1/t_1 + a_2/t_2 = \frac{10}{60} + \frac{9}{60} = \frac{19}{60}$

$T = A/\text{sum} = 60/(2*19) = 30/19 = 1\frac{11}{19}$ hours.

(2) A solution using the fraction button [Ab/c] on the TI-30X IIS calculator.

We want to evaluate:

$$T = \cfrac{\cfrac{1}{2}}{\cfrac{\frac{3}{4}}{4\frac{1}{2}} + \cfrac{\frac{1}{2}}{3\frac{1}{3}}}$$

Here are the button presses:

[1][Ab/c][2][/]

[(][3][Ab/c][4][/][4][Ab/c][1][Ab/c][2][+]

[1][Ab/c][2][/][3][Ab/c][1][Ab/c][3][)]

[=]                                                          display: 1 11/19

So the answer is the same, 1 11/19 hours.

(3) A solution using mental math together with decimals on the TI-30X II S calculator.

[.5][/][(][.75][/][4.5][+][.5][/][3.33][)][=]                1.578199052

Write 1 hour.

[−][1][=][*][60][=]                                          34.69194313

Write 35 minutes.

The answer is 1 hour 35 minutes.

## LESSON 14   ARITHMETIC PUZZLES

Some puzzles are based on simple arithmetic. Sometimes it is even difficult to see why some people are surprised by them or interested in them. But almost anything can be fascinating until it is explained.

### AN EXAMPLE

(1) Write a number that corresponds to the month of your birth (January = 1, . . . , December = 12).

(2) Multiply that number by 4.

(3) Add 12.

(4) Multiply by 25.

(5) Add your age.

(6) Add 13.

(7) Subtract 365.

(8) Add 52.

In this final number, the first digit (or the first 2 digits) is the month of your birth, and the last two (for example, 12 or 07) are your age.

This problem makes a nice calculator exercise in early grades.

Let $m$ be the month, and let $a$ be the age.

| | Keystrokes for the TI-108: |
|---|---|
| (1) Write a number that corresponds to the month of your birth (January = 1, . . . , December = 12). | $[m]$ |
| (2) Multiply that number by 4. | $[*][4]$ |
| (3) Add 12. | $[+][12]$ |
| (4) Multiply by 25. | $[*][25]$ |
| (5) Add your age. | $[+][a]$ |
| (6) Add 13. | $[+][13]$ |
| (7) Subtract 365. | $[-][365]$ |
| (8) Add 52. | $[+][52][=]$ |

The obvious explanation can be provided during the beginning of algebra.

$$(m*4 + 12)*25 = 100*m + 300$$

$$100*m + 300 + a + 13 - 365 + 52 = 100*m + a$$

So if your age is a two-digit number, you see the number of the month followed by your age. If your age is a one-digit number, there is a 0 between them. Finally, if you are more than 100 years old, the trick does not work. So do not show it to your great-grandmother!

## A SECOND EXAMPLE

This simple puzzle uses a four-operation calculator. (The keystrokes given here are for the TI-108.)

| | |
|---|---|
| Enter your age | [age] |
| Take the square of it | [*][=] |
| Add 1 to the result | [+][1][=] |
| Now subtract twice your age | [−][age][=][=] |

Now hand me the calculator, and I'll press just one key and tell you your age.

Solution:

Press $[\sqrt{\ }]$, and mentally add 1 to the answer.

Derivation:

number on display $\quad = age^2 + 1 - 2*age$

$\qquad\qquad\qquad\qquad = age^2 - 2*age + 1$

$\qquad\qquad\qquad\qquad = (age - 1)^2$

and

$\sqrt{((age - 1)^2)} = age - 1$

So:

$age = \sqrt{(\text{number on display})} + 1$

## LESSON 15   THREE NUMBERS PUZZLE

Calculator: TI-30X IIS

Choose three consecutive whole numbers, for example, 21, 22, and 23. Compute the square of the middle number, and subtract from it the product of the other two. Repeat this process a few times with different numbers, until you form a general hypothesis.

### REMARK

Use a calculator. The keystrokes are:

$$[22][x^2][-][\ 21][\times][23][=]$$

Choose three consecutive odd numbers, for example, 35, 37, and 39. Again, compute the square of the middle number, and subtract from it the product of the other two. What do you observe?

### GENERAL SOLUTION

Consider three numbers, $n - m$, $n$, and $n + m$. Compute $n^2 - (n - m)^*(n + m)$.

$$
\begin{aligned}
n^2 - (n - m)^*(n + m) &= n^2 - (n - m)^*n - (n - m)^*m \\
&= n^2 - n^*n + m^*n - n^*m + m^*m \\
&= m^2.
\end{aligned}
$$

Thus the answer does not depend on $n$. In the case of $m = 1$, the value is always 1, and in the case of $m = 2$, the value is 4. This is true for any numbers, not just whole numbers. For example, $(-3.1)^2 - (-4.1)^*(-2.1) = 1$. Here the keystrokes are

$$[(][(-)][3.1][)][x^2][-][(-)][4.1][\times][(-)][2.1][=].$$

## LESSON 16    A POT OF SOUP

From early times, mathematicians have been inventing word problems that are really puzzles solved for amusement, or just as tests of arithmetic skills. Here is one.

Three travelers cooked a pot of soup that they planned to eat the next day. But one traveler got very hungry during the night. So he got up and ate one half of his portion ($\frac{1}{6}$ of the soup in the pot) and went back to sleep.

The second traveler woke up later and wanted to eat one half of his portion. Not knowing that some soup had already been eaten, he ate $\frac{1}{6}$ of the soup left in the pot.

The third traveler slept until morning, but she woke up so hungry that she promptly ate one third of the soup left in the pot, thinking that it was her whole share. When the two other travelers woke up and told their stories, a problem arose: How to divide the soup remaining in the pot so that each person gets one third?

Let students try to work out their own solutions, and then show them the following solution:

## A SOLUTION

We do not know how much soup was in the pot, but let's invent a unit $U$ such that the pot contained exactly 108 $U$ of soup. Thus each traveler should get $\frac{1}{3}$ of 108 $U$, namely 36 $U$ of soup.

The first traveler ate:      $\frac{1}{6}$ * 108 $U$ = 18 $U$ of soup,

and left: 108 $U$ – 18 $U$ = 90 $U$.

The second traveler ate:    $\frac{1}{6}$ * 90 $U$ = 15 $U$ of soup,

and left: 90 $U$ – 15 $U$ = 75 $U$.

The third traveler ate:      $\frac{1}{3}$ * 75 $U$ = 25 $U$ of soup,

and left: 75 $U$ – 25 $U$ = 50 $U$.

Thus the first traveler deserves: 36 $U$ – 18 $U$ = 18 $U$.

The second traveler deserves:    36 $U$ – 15 $U$ = 21 $U$.

The third traveler deserves:      36 $U$ – 25 $U$ = 11 $U$ from the remaining 50 $U$ of soup.

Therefore, the first traveler should get

$^{18}\!/_{50}$ (a little less than $^2\!/_5$).

The second traveler should get

$^{21}\!/_{50}$ (a little more than $^2\!/_5$).

The third traveler should get

$^{11}\!/_{50}$ (a little more than $^1\!/_5$) of the soup that is left.

## REMARKS

The trick of inventing the unit $U$ allows us to solve the problem without messy computation involving fractions. But how to know what trick to use? No particular rules apply, which is what makes the problem challenging. Such problems are often designed in the following way: The author starts with a tricky method and then builds a story around it.

# Arithmetic and Algebra
## Part B:
## Measurement

## LESSON 17   OPEN BOX

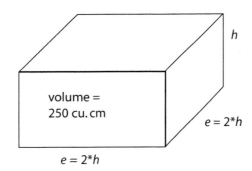

Calculator: TI-108

Design an open box with a square base. Its height should be ½ of its width, and its volume should be 250 cu. cm (¼ liter). Construct the box from poster board.

### DESIGN

If the height of the box is $h$, then the edge $e$ of its square base is $2*h$, and its whole volume $V = e^2*h = (2*h)^2*h = 4*h^3$.

But $V = 250$ cu. cm, so $h$ = cube root of 250/4 = cube root of 62.5 (cm).

Program for the cube root of $x$. (See also the unit titled "Chinese Calendar Box" at http://math.nmsu.edu/breakingaway/.)
Make a guess $z$ for your first approximation. ($z$ must be bigger than zero.)
Press $[x][*][z]$; and repeat $[=][\sqrt{\ }][\sqrt{\ }]$.

Execution for $z = 4$.

| Keystrokes: | Display: | |
|---|---|---|
| [62.5][*][4] | 4. | |
| [=][√ ][√ ] | 3.9763536 | |
| [=][√ ][√ ] | 3.9704638 | |
| [=][√ ][√ ] | 3.9689926 | |
| [=][√ ][√ ] | 3.968625 | |
| [=][√ ][√ ] | 3.9685331 | |
| [=][√ ][√ ] | 3.9685101 | $h = 4.0$ cm (rounded to 1 mm) |
| [*][2][=] | 7.9370202 | $e = 7.9$ cm (rounded to 1 mm) |

The expected volume $V = 4*7.9^2 = 249.64$ cu. cm.

But even if we are very precise in constructing our box, we may make errors of plus or minus 0.05 cm (½ mm) in each of the three dimensions.

Thus $3.95*7.85^2 = 243.4 < V < 4.05*7.95^2 = 256.0$, gives a more reasonable range for the actual volume of the box.

In addition, sides made of poster board are not completely flat, so the estimate that the volume of the box will be somewhere between

245 cu. cm and 255 cu. cm

is quite reasonable.

## REMARK

After drawing plans, students should finish the task by constructing boxes, which are evaluated for accuracy and craftsmanship.

## LESSON 18   THE AREA OF THE SURFACE OF A BOX

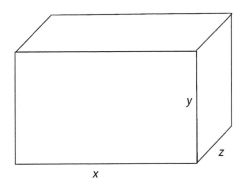

*How to find the surface area of a box with dimensions x, y, and z.*

Each student should bring an empty cereal box (or some other box) to class. The task is to compute the area of its surface.

(1) Formula for the area of the surface

If $x$, $y$, and $z$ are lengths of the edges of a box, its surface area, surface_area, is given by the formula:

$$\text{surface\_area} = 2*(x*y + x*z + y*z).$$

(2) Measurements

Measurements are made in inches and sixteenths of an inch, but they are recorded as decimals. The conversions should be done mentally.

Example:

$x = 2.25$ in.

$y = 6.125$ in.

$z = 8.375$ in.

(3) Preparing a program for a calculator (TI-30X IIS)

It is desirable that each number be entered into the calculator only once. The reason is that entering numbers is one of the main sources of errors.

We rename the variables $A$, $B$, and $C$, and store their values in the calculator.

| Keystrokes: | Display: | |
| --- | --- | --- |
| [2.25][STO][=] | 2.25 → $A$ | 2.25 |
| [6.125][STO][→][=] | 6.125 → $B$ | 6.125 |
| [8.375][STO][→][→][=] | 8.375 → $C$ | 8.375 |

Now we enter the program $2(AB + AC + BC)$. Press [=], and the result is 167.84375.

Answer:

The area of the surface of the box is 168 square inches (more or less).

Keystrokes for the program on the TI-30X IIS:

[2][(][(][MEMVAR][=][MEMVAR][→][=][+][MEMVAR][=][MEMVAR]
[→][→][=][+][MEMVAR][→][=][MEMVAR][→][→][=][)][=]

**LESSON 19   RICE CAKES BOX**

The figure above provides an empty box from white cheddar flavored rice cakes. What is its volume?

## SOLUTION

A solution consists of five steps:

(1) Describe the variables whose values will be measured or computed. We see that the box is a cylinder. So:

    let   $d$        be its diameter, which we will measure;

    let   $r = d/2$   be the radius of the cylinder;

    let   $h$        be its height, also to be measured;

    let   $V$       be its volume, to be computed.

We know that:  $V = \pi * r^2 * h = \pi * (d/2)^2 * h$.

(2) Measure $d$ and $h$.

        $d = 4\frac{1}{2}$ inches

        $h = 9\frac{1}{8}$ inches

(3) Write a program for the TI-30X IIS that computes the value of $V$ for the measured values of $d$ and $h$.

$$[\pi][\times][(][(][4.5][\div][2][)][x^2][\times][9.125][=]$$

(4) Compute the value of $V$.

The program returns 145.1268544.

(5) Write down the answer.

The box has a volume of 145 cubic inches.

## EXTENDING THE LESSON

It is interesting to have students bring different cylinders to class and line them up according to their estimated volumes, and then to line them up according to their computed volumes. (See also lesson 46, "Two Cylinders," in this book.)

# Arithmetic and Algebra
## Part C:
## Other Applications

## LESSON 20   ENGLISH NUMERALS

Calculator: TI-30X IIS

We are going to investigate the meaning of English numerals for whole numbers less than one million, by translating them into arithmetic expressions.

### NUMBER WORDS

The following list contains number words in English for whole numbers less than 1 million, together with their decimal values.

zero = 0

| | | |
|---|---|---|
| one = 1 | ten = 10 | eleven = 11 |
| two = 2 | twenty = 20 | twelve = 12 |
| three = 3 | thirty = 30 | thirteen = 13 |
| four = 4 | forty = 40 | fourteen = 14 |
| five = 5 | fifty = 50 | fifteen = 15 |
| six = 6 | sixty = 60 | sixteen = 16 |
| seven = 7 | seventy = 70 | seventeen = 17 |
| eight = 8 | eighty = 80 | eighteen = 18 |
| nine = 9 | ninety = 90 | nineteen = 19 |

hundred = 100     thousand = 1000

All other English numerals for numbers less than 1 million are combinations of these number words.

### REMARK

We did not include in the list old number words, such as dozen, gross, and score. We also omitted new words such as kilo, which means 1000 in "kilogram," but 1024 in "kilobyte."

### ACTIVITY

A generic example.

(1) Choose a whole number smaller than one million. Say it aloud.

Two hundred seventy-four

(2) Write the decimal value of each number word, leaving large empty spaces between them:

2        100     70       4

(3) Insert the operations + and *, and, if needed, parentheses, ( and ), to form an arithmetic expression that has the same value as the English numeral:

$$2 * 100 + 70 + 4$$

(4) Compute the value of the expression with a calculator.

The keystrokes: $\qquad 2 \times 100 + 70 + 4 = \qquad$ return 274

(5) Read aloud the display to check that you have not made an error.
More examples

One hundred one
$1 * 100 + 1 = 101.$

Two thousand six hundred seventeen
$2 * 1000 + 6 * 100 + 17 = 2,617.$

Twenty-six hundred seventeen
$(20 + 6) * 100 + 17 = 2,617.$

Nine hundred eighty-seven thousand six hundred fifty-four
$(9 * 100 + 80 + 7) * 1000 + 6 * 100 + 50 + 4 = 987,654.$

Create your own examples and study carefully when multiplication is used. (Remember precedence of operations. Multiplication is executed before addition.)

## REMARKS

- Numbers that are used for some reason other than their values, for example, phone numbers, are often read differently. For example, 4495092 can be read "four, four, nine, five, zero, nine, two," or more likely, "four, four, nine, fifty, ninety-two."

- The preceding activity can be extended to less standard numerals.
Examples:

Four score and seven years ago . . .
$4 * 20 + 7 = 87$

Four and twenty blackbirds . . .
$4 + 20 = 24$

Five and a half dozen eggs . . .
$(5 + 1/2) * 12 = 66$

## LESSON 21   WHOLE NUMBERS WRITTEN IN BASE 2

This way of introducing base 2 stresses that it is just a different representation of familiar numbers and not a new kind of numbers, such as, for example, imaginary numbers. It also provides some calculator and mental exercises.

An algorithm that converts a whole number, $n > 0$, from decimal notation to binary notation.

- Enter $n$ into the calculator: $[n]$

- Next, write 0 or 1 from right to left, repeating the following:
    If the number is odd, write 1, and subtract 1 by pressing $[-][1][=]$.
    If the number is even write 0.
  Divide the number by 2: $[/][2][=]$

- When the display shows 0, you are finished. You have the number in binary notation.

### REMARK

Some keystrokes can be omitted in this sequence, but it is not recommended, because logical clarity is more important than efficiency.

### EXAMPLE

($n = 11$)

| Keystrokes: | Display: | Binary digits: |
|---|---|---|
| [11] | 11. | 1 |
| [−][1][=] | 10. | |
| [/][2][=] | 5. | 11 |
| [−][1][=] | 4. | |
| [/][2][=] | 2. | 011 |
| [/][2][=] | 1. | 1011 |
| [−][1][=] | 0. | |

So 11 written in decimal notation is 1011 written in binary notation.

Simplified keystrokes:

| [11] | 11. | 1 |
|---|---|---|
| [−][1][/][2][=] | 5. | 11 |
| [−][1][/][2][=] | 2. | 011 |
| [=] | 1. | 1011 |

Children should choose the numbers to be converted. Each conversion should be done by at least two children to avoid errors. The results should be displayed on the blackboard in the form of a table.

## EXAMPLE

| English: | Decimal: | Binary: |
|---|---|---|
| zero | 0 | 0 |
| one | 1 | 1 |
| two | 2 | 10 |
| seven | 7 | 111 |
| eleven | 11 | 1011 |
| seventeen | 17 | 10001 |
| eighteen | 18 | 10010 |
| nineteen | 19 | 10011 |
| thirty-two | 32 | 100000 |
| one thousand two | 1002 | 1111101010 |
| ... | ... | ... |

## REMARK

In a multilingual classroom additional columns for other languages may be added.

## LESSON 22   FIBONACCI SURPRISE

Calculator: TI-108. (You may use any other calculator, but you need to be able to compute the Fibonacci numbers.)

### SUMMARY

The following program computes the Fibonacci sequence:

> [1][+][1][=]
> Repeat: [+][=]

Each student in the class will compute his or her own sequence by choosing two initial numbers $A$ and $B$, instead of 1 and 1, and then proceed as above.

    The ratios of two large consecutive numbers of the students' sequences will be computed, and the results will be compared, discussed, and displayed.

### TASK

(1) Choose two whole numbers $A$ and $B$ between 1 and 100. Write them down.

(2) Execute the program:

> [A][+][B][=]
>
> Repeat: [+][=]

until the display shows a number greater than one million.
Call this number $C$ and write it down.
Press:

> [M+][+][=];

write the answer down, and call it $D$.
Finally, compute the quotient $D/C$ by pressing:

> [÷][MRC][=].

All your results should be neatly written down, because they will be compared to the results of other students and displayed. Do not forget to write down your name.

An example of a student's results, shown on one half page.

> My numbers                              by Mary S.
> Start:
> > $A = 71$
> > $B = 17$
> Finish:
> > $C = 1078253$
> > $D = 1744650$
> Quotient:
> > $D/C = 1.6180339$

## SURPRISE

What is the surprise? All students get the same quotient!

## DISCUSSION

(1) What is this quotient?

The golden ratio: $(\sqrt{5} + 1)/2$

Press [5][$\sqrt{\ }$][+][1][÷][2][=] and see: 1.6180339.

(2) Why is this so?
Any three consecutive numbers $x, y, z$ from above are related by the equation:

$x + y = z.$

Therefore, their quotients $y/x$ and $z/y$ are related as follows:

$x/y + 1 = z/y,$

which can be rewritten as:

$1 + y/x = (y/x)^*(z/y).$

But if the ratios of two consecutive numbers converge to some number $r$, then $y/x \rightarrow r$, and $z/y \rightarrow r$. Thus:

$1 + r = r^*r.$

The number $r$ must be positive, so the ratio $r$, approximated by $D/C$, is the positive solution of the equation:

$$r^2 - r - 1 = 0.$$

Its positive solution is $(\sqrt{5} + 1)/2$.
Thus, it is not surprising that everyone got the same number.

## REMARKS

- The conclusions about limits based on their approximations are valid only when these limits exist. So if the ratios of two consecutive numbers of our sequences were not convergent, any conclusions about $r$ would be meaningless. A rigorous mathematical proof of the convergence is of course possible, but it is beyond the scope of this lesson.

- This lesson may be taught in early grades without the final explanation. The fact that the "final" ratio $D/C$ does not depend on the choice of the initial numbers $A$ and $B$ would remain an empirical observation.

## LESSON 23  FRACTION GAME USING THE CONTINUED FRACTION ALGORITHM

Calculator: TI-108

The game is played as follows. One player chooses a (proper) fraction with a reasonably small denominator, and converts it into a decimal using a four-operation calculator. This decimal is given to the other players, who try to reconstruct the original fraction (in its lowest terms).

With one-digit denominators, the game can be played as a guess-and-check game. With two-digit denominators, it is already difficult if the players do not know some special techniques. The game can be played with denominators up to three digits. For bigger denominators, different fractions can lead to the same eight-digit decimal.

This game can be played as an introduction to the continued fraction algorithm, which allows you to convert decimals into common fractions in a regular way. Of course the continued fraction algorithm removes any challenge from the game. But using the game as an introduction shows that the continued fraction algorithm solves otherwise difficult problems.

### THE CONTINUED FRACTION ALGORITHM

The derivation, the proof of correctness, and the relation to the Euclid algorithm for finding the greatest common divisor, for the continued fraction algorithm, are too complex to be discussed in early grades. What can be presented is the algorithm itself, its properties, and its applications. Its pedagogical value lies in combining written, mental, and calculator computations. Its practical value is in the efficient processing of common fractions, and its mathematical value is in its systematic approach to approximations.

### WHAT DOES THE CONTINUED FRACTION ALGORITHM DO?

Given a positive decimal (a positive real number) the continued fraction algorithm provides a sequence of better and better approximations by common fractions. If we start with a decimal version of a common fraction and carry out the computation without rounding errors, the original fraction is restored.

### AN EXAMPLE

Let the number be 3.1415926 (it is an approximation of pi).
Prepare a data sheet.

| coefficients: | | |
|---|---|---|
| numerators: | 1 | |
| denominators: | 0 | 1 |
| fractions: | | |

- Enter the decimal into the calculator:

  [3.1415926][M+]                display: 3.1415926

- Write the whole part of the decimal, 3, in the second column.

  (If the number is smaller than 1, its whole part is 0.)

  The first approximation is the whole number 3/1 = 3.

| coefficients: | | |
|---|---|---|
| numerators: | 1 | 3 |
| denominators: | 0 | 1 |
| fractions: | | 3/1 |

- Subtract the whole part and take the reciprocal:

  [–][3][/][=]          display: 7.0625159

  Write the whole part as a coefficient in the third column.

- Multiply it by the last numerator and add the previous numerator:

  7*3 + 1 = 22

  Write it as the numerator in the third column.

- Multiply the coefficient by the last denominator and add the previous denominator:

  7*1 + 0 = 7

  Write it as the denominator in the third column.

- The second approximation is 22/7.

| coefficients: | | | 7 |
|---|---|---|---|
| numerators: | 1 | 3 | 22 |
| denominators: | 0 | 1 | 7 |
| fractions: | | 3/1 | 22/7 |

- Subtract the whole part and take the reciprocal:

  [–][7][/][=]          display: 15.99593

  Write the whole part as a coefficient in the fourth column.

- Multiply it by the last numerator and add the previous numerator:

  15*22 + 3 = 333 (You may use another calculator to do it.)

Write it as the numerator in the fourth column.

- Multiply the coefficient by the last denominator and add the previous denominator:

  15*7 + 1 = 106

Write it as the denominator in the fourth column.

- The third approximation is 333/106.

| | | | 7 | 15 |
|---|---|---|---|---|
| coefficients: | | | 7 | 15 |
| numerators: | 1 | 3 | 22 | 333 |
| denominators: | 0 | 1 | 7 | 106 |
| fractions: | | 3/1 | 22/7 | 333/106 |

- Subtract the whole part and take the reciprocal:

  [–][15][/][=]          display: 1.0040866

Write the whole part as a coefficient in the fifth column.

- Multiply it by the last numerator and add the previous numerator:

  1*333 + 22 = 355

Write it as the numerator in the fifth column.

- Multiply the coefficient by the last denominator and add the previous denominator:

  1*106 + 7 = 113

Write it as the denominator in the fifth column.

- The fourth approximation is 355/113.

| | | | 7 | 15 | 1 |
|---|---|---|---|---|---|
| coefficients: | | | 7 | 15 | 1 |
| numerators: | 1 | 3 | 22 | 333 | 355 |
| denominators: | 0 | 1 | 7 | 106 | 113 |
| fractions: | | 3/1 | 22/7 | 333/106 | 355/113 |

- Subtract the whole part and take the reciprocal:

  [–][1][/][=]          display: 244.70219

Write the whole part as a coefficient in the sixth column.

- Multiply it by last numerator and add the previous numerator:

  244*355 + 333 = 86953

Write it as the numerator in the sixth column.

- Multiply the coefficient by the last denominator and add the previous denominator:

  244*113 + 106 = 27678

Write it as the denominator in the sixth column.

- The fifth approximation is 86953/27678.

| coefficients: | | | 7 | 15 | 1 | 244 |
|---|---|---|---|---|---|---|
| numerators: | 1 | 3 | 22 | 333 | 355 | 86953 |
| denominators: | 0 | 1 | 7 | 106 | 113 | 27678 |
| fractions: | | 3/1 | 22/7 | 333/106 | 355/113 | 86953/27678 |

## APPROXIMATIONS

Let's determine how close each consecutive approximation is to the original 3.1415926. We will compute the difference, and the percentage of error.

| Keystrokes: | Difference: | Keystrokes: | Percentage: |
|---|---|---|---|
| [3.1415926][M+] | | | |
| [3][–][MRC][=] | –0.1415926 | [/][MRC][%] | –4.5% |
| [22][/][7][–][MRC][=] | 0.0012645 | [/][MRC][%] | 0.04% |
| [333][/][106][–][MRC][=] | –0.0000832 | [/][MRC][%] | –0.003% |
| [355][/][113][–][MRC][=] | 0.0000003 | [/][MRC][%] | 0.00001% |
| [86953][/][27678] | | | |
|     [–][MRC][=] | 0 | | |

In this range of denominators and numerators, many fractions, when truncated to eight decimal digits, yield 3.1415926. For example, 87308/27791 = 3.1415926.

## ANOTHER EXAMPLE

Let's begin with the fraction 17/91. We change it to a decimal:

    [17][/][91][=] gives 0.1868131
    which is a decimal approximation to 17/91.

We want to change the decimal back to 17/91 using the continued fraction algorithm. Here are the keystrokes:

| [/][=] | 5.3529436 | Take the reciprocal and write the whole part in the table. |
| [−][5][=] | .3529436 | Subtract off the whole part. |
| [/][=] | 2.8333138 | Take the reciprocal and write the whole part in the table. |
| [−][2][=] | .8333138 | Subtract off the whole part. |
| [/][=] | 1.2000281 | Take the reciprocal and write the whole part in the table. |
| [−][1][=] | .2000281 | Subtract off the whole part. |
| [/][=] | 4.9992975 | Take the reciprocal and write the whole part in the table. |
| [−][4][=] | .9992975 | Subtract off the whole part. |
| [/][=] | 1.0007029 | Take the reciprocal and write the whole part in the table. |
| [−][1][=] | .0007029 | Subtract off the whole part. |
| [/][=] | 1422.6774 | Take the reciprocal and write the whole part in the table. |

Here is the table we formed:

| coefficients: | | 5 | 2 | 1 | 4 | 1 | 1422 | 1 |
|---|---|---|---|---|---|---|---|---|
| 1 | 0 | 1 | 2 | 3 | 14 | 17 | 24188 | 24205 |
| 0 | 1 | 5 | 11 | 16 | 75 | 91 | 129477 | 129568 |
| fractions: | | 1/5 | 2/11 | 3/16 | 14/75 | 17/91 | 24188/12977 | 24205/129568 |

Notice that:

[17][/][91][=] gives 0.1868131,

[24188][/][129477][=] gives 0.1868131, and

[24205][/][129568][=] gives 0.1868131.

And here is 17/91 written as a continued fraction:

$$\frac{17}{91} = \cfrac{1}{5 + \cfrac{1}{2 + \cfrac{1}{1 + \cfrac{1}{5}}}}$$

# Two-Dimensional Geometry

## LESSON 24 FIVE-PETAL ROSETTE

This lesson has been taught in grades one through eight.

### TOOLS

Compass, protractor, sheet of paper, crayons or colored pencils, scissors (optional)

### TASK

Using a compass, draw a fairly large circle on a sheet of paper. Using a protractor, make 5 equally spaced tick marks on it on its border. Because 360 ÷ 5 = 72, the tick marks should be 72 degrees apart.

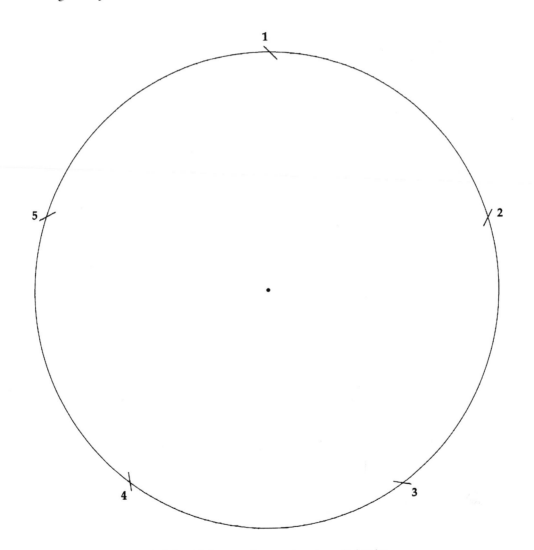

*A circle with five equally spaced marks on its border.*

Now set your compass to have a radius that is the distance between two consecutive tick marks. Use each tick mark as a center, and draw five different arcs. For example, with the compass point at tick mark 1, join 5 and 2 with an arc. With the compass point at tick mark 2, join 1 and 3. Continuing, join 2 and 4, and then 3 and 5, and finally 4 and 1.

You have a big rosette inside the circle, and a small one inside the big one.

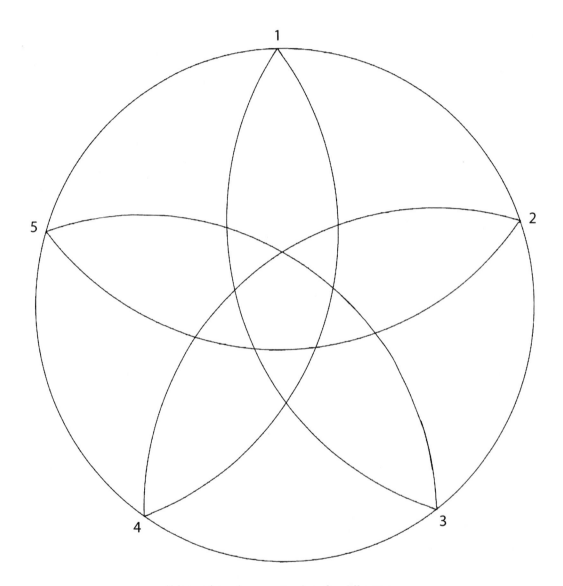

*Using each mark as a center, draw five different arcs.*

Color them with crayons or colored pencils, and, if you want, cut out the circle.

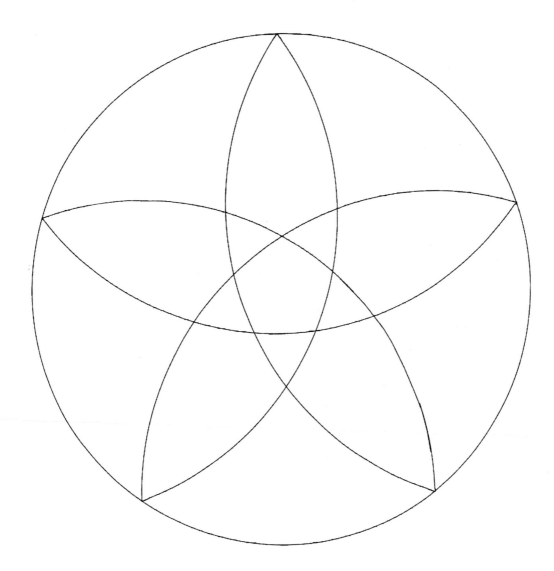

*A five-petal rosette, ready to color and cut out.*

## LESSON 25   SHAMROCK

This unit has been taught in first grade and up.

### SOME HISTORY

St. Patrick's Day is celebrated on March 17 in honor of the patron saint of Ireland. His death on March 17, in about A.D. 461, has been observed in the United States since colonial days. Observance of the day since 1845 has become nationwide. It is celebrated in homes, churches, schools, and places of entertainment. Merchants sell special wearing apparel, flowers, shamrocks, and greeting cards. Some cities hold St. Patrick's Day parades.

Many stories about Patrick are based only on legend. One of the best-known tales tells how he charmed the snakes of Ireland into the sea so they were drowned. According to another legend, Patrick used a three-leaf shamrock to illustrate the idea of the Trinity, and he planted it in Ireland. Many people believe that the shamrock came to be the traditional symbol of Ireland as a result of this legend.

The shamrock is the national flower of Ireland (Eire). The name *shamrock* is anglicized from Seamrog, which means trefoil (three-leaved). It is given to a number of plants, but a small clover is usually considered the true shamrock. Its leaves have a blue-green color. Black medic, nonesuch, yellow trefoil, and hop clover have been called shamrocks. The shamrock appears with the thistle and the rose on the British coat of arms, because these are the national flowers of Ireland, Scotland, and England. Some authorities say the wood sorrel is the true shamrock. Its leaves are like those of the white clover.*

### ACTIVITIES

(1) Drawing a (stylized) shamrock

Supplies: Poster board or card stock or construction paper (green!), ruler, compass, protractor (optional), scissors, calculator

- Draw an equilateral triangle. A nice length for the edge is 3 inches. Around each vertex of the triangle you are going to draw a circle with radius half the length of the edge (so here, for example, your circle will have a 1.5-inch radius). Be sure to draw your triangle far enough from the border of your paper so that you can draw the circle. To draw the equilateral triangle, you may use a ruler to draw the first edge, and then measure the edge and set your compass to that radius. Put the point of your compass on one end of the edge and swing an arc. Do the same thing on the other end of the edge. Where the two arcs meet is the third vertex of your triangle. Finish drawing the triangle.

- Set the radius of your compass at ½ the length of your triangle's edge. Draw three circles, each with a center on a vertex of the triangle. If you do it correctly, each circle will just touch (be tangent to) the other two circles. This shape is called a trefoil.

- Hand-draw a stem on your shamrock.

*This information was taken mainly from *The World Book Encyclopedia* (1979), Chicago, IL: World Book-Childcraft International Inc.

(2) Design and make a four-leaf shamrock (begin with a square instead of a triangle)

So that it will fit on your cardstock, you may use an edge length of 2 inches (not 3). You may make a hole in a leaf or in the stem for a piece of yarn using a paper punch, and wear the shamrock as a bracelet or necklace.

(3) In higher grades, the shamrock is challenging to draw using Geometer's Sketchpad. (See the three-leaf and four-leaf shamrocks below.)

*Three circles, each with a center on the vertex of the triangle, form a trefoil.*

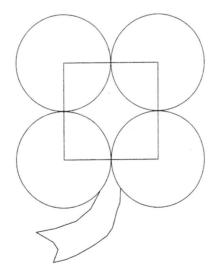

*A four-leaf shamrock consists of four circles, each with a center on the vertex of a square.*

## LESSON 26   YIN AND YANG, AGAIN AND AGAIN!

Previously we learned about the Yin and Yang symbol (see *Breaking Away from the Math Book II*). In this unit we will design, color, and cut out the pattern below:

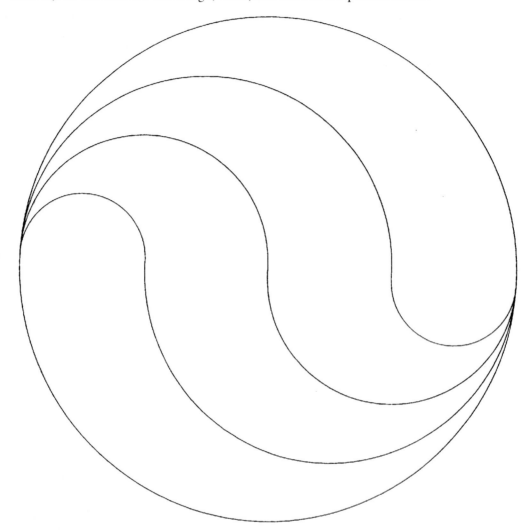

*A Yin Yang design ready to be colored and cut out to form a jigsaw puzzle.*

## SUPPLIES

Paper, compass, ruler, scissors, markers or colored pencils

(1)  Draw a large circle. A diameter of eight inches is easy to work with, and we will assume this diameter.

(2)  Draw the diameter of the circle.

(3) Measure the diameter, and put tick marks along it at ⅛ its length, ¼, ⅜, ⅝, ¾, and ⅞ of its length (at one, two, three, five, six, and seven inches).

(4) Place the point of your compass at the ⅛ mark, and open the compass to a radius of one inch. Draw a half circle.

(5) Place the point of the compass at the ⅞ mark and draw another half circle, on the other side of the diameter.

(6) With the point of your compass at the ¼ mark, and with the compass open to a two-inch radius, draw another half circle, over the first one you drew.

(7) With the point of the compass at the ¾ mark, draw a half circle over the second one you drew.

(8) With the point of the compass at the ⅜ mark and with a three inch radius, draw a half circle over the first and third ones you drew.

(9) With the point at the ⅝ mark, draw a half circle over the second and fourth ones you drew.

(10) Erase the diameter, and color the four sections of the circle.

(11) (optional) Cut them out, and you have a nice jigsaw puzzle.


## QUESTION

What percentage of the area of the whole circle is each of the pieces? (25%) Can you prove it?

## LESSON 27    BISHOP'S CAP

This puzzle has six congruent pieces, each one looking like a Bishop's cap (see figure below).

*The Bishop's cap puzzle consists of six congruent pieces.*

Draw a circle and then lightly draw six more circles with the same radius, whose centers are equally spaced one radius apart on the first circle's circumference, as in the figure below.

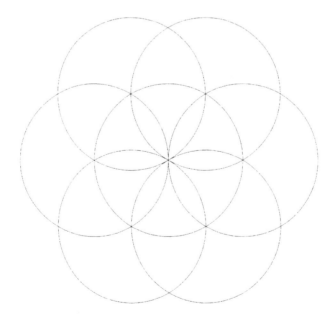

*You begin the Bishop's cap puzzle design with seven circles, as shown.*

Erase the center circle entirely, as well as parts of the arcs of the six circles on the outside of the drawing, as shown in the figure below.

*Erase the entire center circle, together with parts of the arcs of six of the circles, as shown.*

Next erase some arcs on the interior, as shown in the figure below.

*Erase some arcs on the interior, as shown, and the puzzle is ready to color and cut out.*

Now color the six Bishop's caps. Finally, cut out the six pieces and arrange them into different patterns. One thing you can do is make two circles out of them, as shown in the figures below!

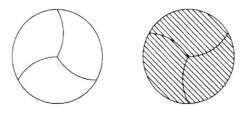

*The six Bishops' caps may be arranged into many designs, including two circles!*

Now rearrange them back into their original shape.

## LESSON 28    IRREGULAR POLYGONS

In this class project, students will need many colored, rather small squares of paper. The squares must be the same color on both sides. The best material is a colored "note cube" which contains 550 3-1/2 by 3-1/2 inch squares in 11 bright colors.

A large poster-size sheet of brown packing paper put on a wall may serve as a poster to which students will glue or tape their polygons.

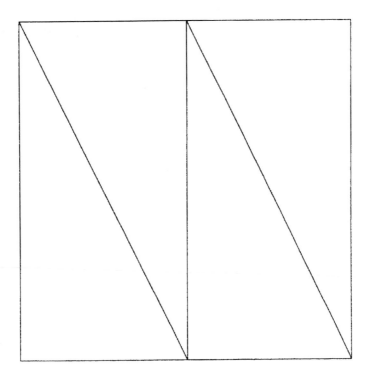

*Four right triangles with legs of 1³⁄₄ and 3¹⁄₂ inches, made from a 3¹⁄₂ by 3¹⁄₂ inch square.*

## THE PROJECT

Students cut their squares into four right triangles with legs of 1¾ and 3½ inches (as in the figure above).

## TASK

Make as many different polygons as you can by joining two, three, or four triangles (of the same color). Fix your figure together with Scotch tape, and glue or tape it to the poster.

Be sure that you check that a polygon of the same shape and size is not already on the poster!

## GROUND RULES

The triangles are joined by edges. The edges have to match exactly. One short leg of a triangle may be joined only with a short leg of another triangle, and so on. But you may turn triangles on the other side.

Here are two polygons, each made from two triangles.

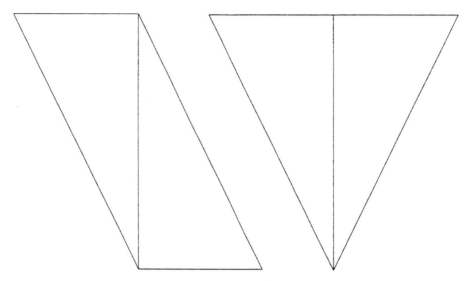

*Two polygons, a parallelogram and a triangle, each made from two triangles.*

The first one is a parallelogram, and the second one is a triangle.

## REMARKS

How much geometrical terminology is introduced is not very important, but some concepts are important.

(1) Polygon

Do not give a definition, but say that:

- all sides of a polygon are straight segments.

- some of the corners may be turned inwards (technically this means that a polygon does not have to be convex).

- to determine the number of sides, it is better to count corners. Notice that the second polygon shown is a triangle, even if one of its sides was made from two legs of two smaller right triangles.

(2) Congruence

We say that two geometric figures are congruent when they have the same shape and size. In geometry we often shorten this to just one word: *same*.

In order to check to see whether two plane figures are congruent, try to put one on top of the other. If you can make them fit exactly, they are congruent. In doing so, you may turn a figure on the other side.

You can make six different polygons from two triangles, 10 from three triangles, and 65 from four triangles. So do not insist that students find all of them!

When the number of polygons on the poster increases, checking whether a new one is not congruent (not the same) as one already on the poster becomes difficult. Special attention should be given to this part of the project. And it is better if checking is done, not by individual children, but by small groups.

Whether the design of the polygons is done individually or in groups does not matter, as long as all children participate in all phases of the project.

If some care is taken about spacing the polygons on the poster, and about the pattern of colors that emerges, the display can be impressive.

## LESSON 29 STAR MAKER

The star maker kit is a puzzle that contains 12 right triangles (see the figures below):

Four right triangles with legs 1 and 3 units long: (1, 3)-triangles

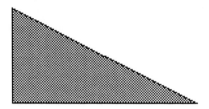

Four right triangles with legs 1 and 2 units long: (1, 2)-triangles

And four right isosceles triangles with legs 1 and 1 units long: (1, 1)-triangles

We call a star a configuration of pieces that contains exactly one point, not on its border, in which all the pieces meet.

Examples of problems (see the figure below with three stars).

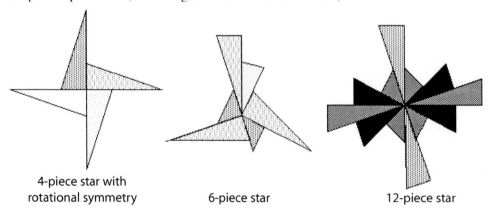

4-piece star with rotational symmetry

6-piece star

12-piece star

*Stars made from 4, 6, and 12 pieces.*

- Make a star from 4, 5, 6, 7, 8, 9, 10, 11, and all 12 pieces.

- Make two identical stars, each one from 6 pieces.

- Make stars that have rotational symmetry.

This kit is also good for making other designs in addition to stars.

## MAKING A KIT

Students work individually or in small groups. Each group (or individual) gets two colored 3- by 5-inch index cards.

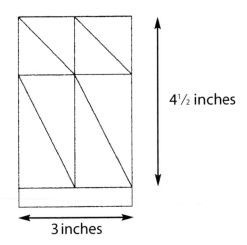

4½ inches

3 inches

*Four (1, 1)-triangles and four (1, 2)-triangles are made from a 3- by 5-inch index card.*

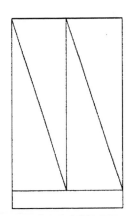

*Four (1, 3)-triangles are made from a 3- by 5-inch index card.*

Taking 1.5 inches as the unit, they make four (1, 3)-triangles from one card, and the remaining eight triangles from the other card (see the figure above, left). They should exchange some triangles so that each group has triangles of three different colors.

## STUDYING THE KIT

After students make many stars, the question may be posed. "Why is this kit so good for making stars?" The answer is simple. Observe that:

(1) The two smaller acute angles of a (1, 2)-triangle and a (1, 3)-triangle add up to 45°.

(2) The two bigger acute angles of a (1, 2)-triangle and a (1, 3)-triangle add up to 135°.

These facts are responsible for the amazing variety of ways a full circle can be filled with the angles of the triangles from this kit. Of course the fact that the legs of all the triangles have ratios 1 to 2 to 3 allows the pieces to fit together in many other patterns.

## SOME TRIGONOMETRY

For this part, students should use the TI-30X IIS, or another calculator of similar power. Question: Are observations (1) and (2) exact, or only approximate?

> For a (1, 2)-triangle, the tangents of its acute angles are ½ and 2.
>
> For a (1, 3)-triangle, the tangents of its acute angles are ⅓ and 3.

But:

| | |
|---|---|
| arctan ½ = 26.56505118 deg | arctan 2 = 63.43494882 deg |
| arctan ⅓ = 18.43494882 deg | arctan 3 = 71.56505118 deg |
| sum = 45 deg | sum = 135 deg |

These results are not a proof of facts (1) and (2), but they give a good indication that such a proof may be found. In addition, from a practical point of view, they establish (1) and (2) as empirical facts, because any possible differences cannot be bigger than 0.00000001 of one degree!

But are observations (1) and (2) independent of each other? No. The sum of the angles in a triangle is 180 degrees. Thus the sum of the angles in two right triangles is 360 degrees. Two right angles account for 180 degrees. So if two smaller acute angles sum to 45 degrees, then the remaining two angles sum to 360 – 180 – 45 = 135 degrees.

Facts (1) and (2) are surprising, but we should be surprised only once, because one of them is an easy conclusion from the other one.

## REMARK

Many people, including some mathematicians, think that mathematical proofs establish the truth of mathematical theorems. A more modern point of view is different: mathematical proofs establish relations between different mathematical statements. We have not proved either (1) or (2). But we proved that one follows from the other.

## USES OF THE STAR-MAKER KIT

The star-maker kit consists of three kinds of right triangles, (1, 1), (2, 1), and (3, 1). (The numbers describe the lengths of the legs of these triangles, measured in an arbitrary unit.) If we call the smaller of their acute angles $A_1$, $A_2$, and $A_3$, and the bigger ones $B_1$, $B_2$, and $B_3$ (actually, $A_1 = B_1 = 45°$ for the (1, 1) triangle), then:

$$A_1 + A_2 + A_3 = 90°$$

and:

$$B_1 + B_2 + B_3 = 180°.$$

This property allows us to build a large variety of "stars" because of the many ways a complete angle of 360 degrees can be formed from these angles.

But all the legs of these triangles are commensurable, and their ratios are ratios of the small whole numbers 1, 2, and 3. This fact allows us to create many other interesting patterns, especially convex polygons.

Other interesting numerical dependencies can be noted among the lengths of the sides. The hypotenuses have lengths:

$$\sqrt{2}, \ \sqrt{5} \ \text{and} \ \sqrt{10}.$$

So the following proportions hold:

$$1/(\sqrt{2}) = (\sqrt{5})/(\sqrt{10})$$
$$1/(\sqrt{5}) = (\sqrt{2})/(\sqrt{10})$$

In addition, $\sqrt{5} + 1 = 3.236\ldots$, which is very close to $\sqrt{10} = 3.1622\ldots$, so these lengths may be used in some approximate constructions.

## GROUND RULES FOR MAKING POLYGONS

When matching edges, only the total length counts. Thus, for example, two edges of length 2 can be matched with an edge of length 1 and one of length 3.

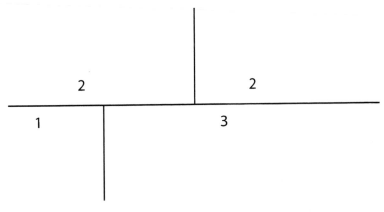

*When you build polygons, you match total lengths, so two edges of length 2 can be matched with an edge length of 1 and one of 3.*

## Task 1

Make squares having areas of 1, 2, 4, 5, 9, and 10 square units (see the figurebelow).

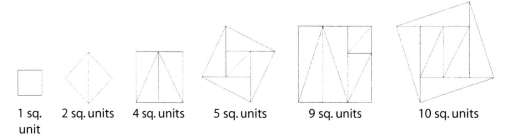

1 sq. unit  2 sq. units  4 sq. units  5 sq. units  9 sq. units  10 sq. units

*Squares with areas 1, 2, 4, 9, and 10 square units, built from the kit.*

## Task 2

Make rectangles having areas of 3, 6, and 12 square units.

## Task 3

Make a parallelogram having an area of 7 square units (see the figure below).

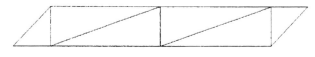

*A parallelogram with area 7 square units.*

## Task 4

Make triangles of different sizes and shapes.

## Task 5

Make convex polygons of different shapes and sizes (see the figure below).

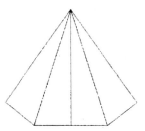

*A convex polygon made from four congruent pieces.*

## LESSON 30    WHAT IS A RHOMBUS?

This unit has been taught in middle school.
Dividing a hexagon into rhombuses can be done in early grades (see the unit titled "Snowflake" in *Breaking Away from the Math Book II*).

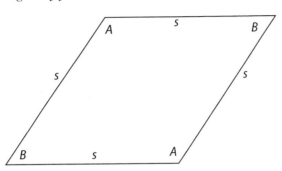

A rhombus has four equal sides, just like a square, but its angles do not have to be right angles. So we have rhombuses (or rhombi) of different shapes. Actually you may call a square a "right rhombus."

Each rhombus has its opposite sides parallel to each other, and its opposite angles are equal. The two adjacent angles $A$ and $B$ add up to 180 degrees. Thus the shape and size of a rhombus are completely determined by two values, the length of its side $s$, and one of the angles, either $A$ or $B$ (see the figure above).

## ACTIVITIES

### Part 1

Every regular polygon with an even number of sides, $2*n$, of length $s$, can be cut into rhombuses with sides $s$, and having angles that are multiples of $180/n$.

To make a polygon cut up into rhombuses from poster board:

(1) Draw a regular polygon with $2*n$ sides. Each side should have a length of 2 inches or more. (We have taught this by beginning with a circle, and inscribing the polygon in the circle.)

(2) Divide it into rhombuses with sides $s$. For $n > 4$, such a partition can be done in many ways.

(3) You may cut the pieces out and keep them in an envelope. You have a nice puzzle, and the pieces can be used to form many other attractive shapes.

Of course you do not need to cut the pieces out. You get a lovely piece of art when you simply color them! (See the large figures at the end of part 1.)

Drawing and cutting out pieces requires high precision, and the difficulty increases fast with n. So be sure that students have good quality tools and adequate skills for the task.

*Tools*: Rulers, compasses, protractors, scissors, sharp pencils (pencils of hardness 3 or 4 are better). Markers or colored pencils (if you plan to color!). Calculators are optional because all calculations can be done mentally.

(1) An octagon is divided into four rhombuses with angle $A$ = 45 degrees, and two with angle $A$ = 90 degrees (squares). (See illustration in figure below.)

(2) A decagon is divided into five rhombuses with angle $A$ = 36 degrees, and five with angle $A$ = 72 degrees. (See illustration in figure below.)

(3) A dodecagon is divided into six rhombuses with angle $A$ = 30 degrees, six with angle $A$ = 60 degrees, and three with angle $A$ = 90 degrees (squares). (See illustration in figure below.)

A hexagon splits into three rhombuses, which is simple but surprising to young children. (See illustration in figure below.)

And polygons with more than 12 sides may be too difficult to handle in a classroom. In general a polygon having $2*n$ sides splits into $n*(n-1)/2$ rhombuses.

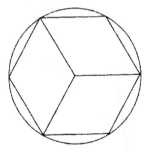

A regular hexagon splits into three rhombuses.

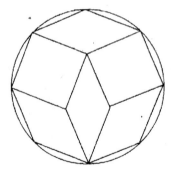

A regular octagon splits into six rhombuses.

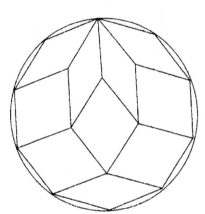

A regular decagon splits into ten rhombuses.

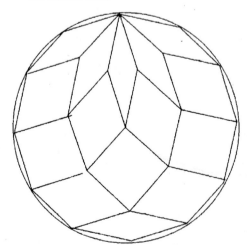

A regular dodecagon splits into 15 rhombuses.

*Splitting a regular hexagon, octagon, decagon, and dodecagon into rhombuses.*

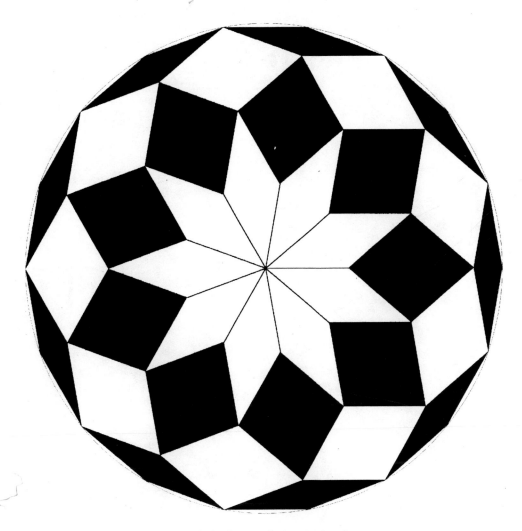

*An 18-sided polygon splits into 36 rhombuses.*

Another way to split an 18-gon into 36 rhombuses.

## Part 2

If the regular polygon has an odd number of sides, then it can be divided into isosceles triangles. (See the figure below.)

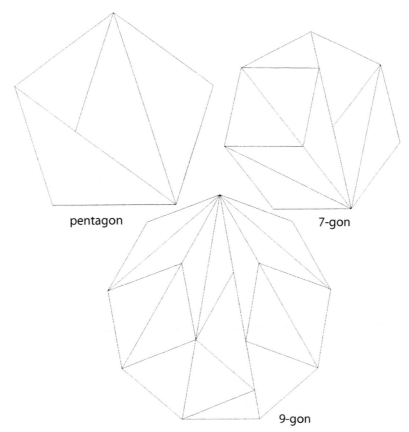

*Splitting a regular pentagon, 7-gon, and 9-gon into isosceles triangles.*

A pentagon splits into four isosceles triangles; a 7-gon splits into 9; and a 9-gon splits into 16.

## REFERENCE

Frederickson, Greg N. (1997). *Dissections Plane & Fancy*. Cambridge: Cambridge University Press, pages 10–11.

## LESSON 31    QUADRILATERAL JIGSAW PUZZLE: EARLY GEOMETRY

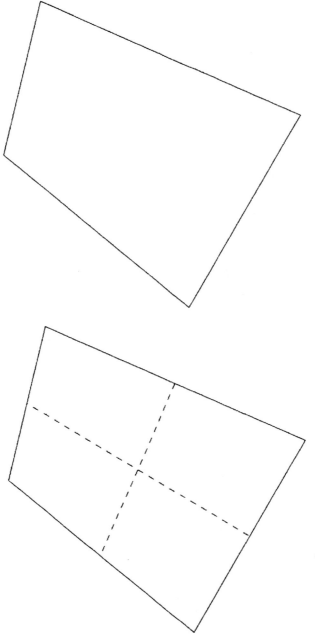

### ACTIVITY

(1) Draw a fairly large, irregular convex quadrilateral, on a piece of rather stiff paper or (even better) on a piece of poster board that is colored only on one side.

(2) Connect the middle points of the opposite sides with straight lines. They divide the whole figure into four smaller quadrilaterals.

(3) Cut them out, getting a four-piece puzzle.

(4) Notice that you can put these pieces together in two different ways to form one large quadrilateral. (The edges of the small quadrilaterals form the edges of one of the quadrilaterals [the one you started with]. For the second quadrilateral, they form the central lines. [See the figures below.])

(5) (For older students) Can you show that the quadrilateral in the figure below (at right) is a parallelogram? One way to determine whether a quadrilateral is a parallelogram is to see if its opposite angles are equal.

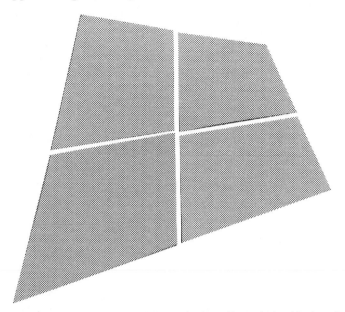

*An irregular convex quadrilateral. The midpoints of its opposite sides have been connected by straight lines, and it has been cut into four smaller quadrilaterals.*

*A new quadrilateral made from the four pieces in the figure at the left. Can you show that it is a parallelogram?*

## REMARKS

(1) A suggested way to find the middle point of a side.

- Measure the side in centimeters and millimeters.

- Divide the number by 2, using a calculator.

- Using the ruler again, mark on the side a point at this distance from one of the corners. (This step is the most difficult part of the lesson.)

(2) To save poster board, the teacher may prepare and cut out big quadrilaterals and give them to students, who do only steps 2, 3, and 4 of the activity.

(3) Students should be introduced to the word *quadrilateral*, which can be written on the blackboard. However, they should be allowed to use the word *quad*.

## LESSON 32   THREE SQUARES

In ancient Egypt, surveyors and architects constructed right angles using a loop of rope 12 units long, with three knots tied at distances of 3, 4, and 5 units. If such a loop is stretched, it forms a right triangle, because 32 + 42 = 52. This method of forming a right triangle was a precursor of the famous Pythagorean theorem.

### TASK

Take a square, 5 by 5 inches. Dissect it into four pieces, each consisting of a whole number of unit squares, so that you may form from these pieces two squares, one 3 by 3 inches and the other 4 by 4 inches. (See the figure below.)

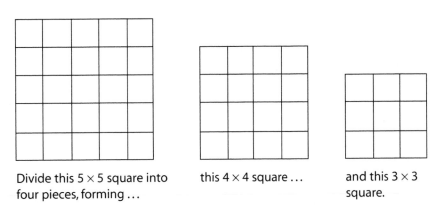

Divide this 5 × 5 square into four pieces, forming …

this 4 × 4 square …

and this 3 × 3 square.

At least two solutions should be discussed in the class. Students should know that one of the four pieces may be one of the target squares (i.e., a 3 × 3 square or a 4 × 4 square), but it doesn't have to be.

### FOLLOW-UP

Find at least two solutions to the puzzle that were not discussed in class. Make one of them from a 5- by 8-inch index card. Bring your solutions to class to show to others.

### SOLUTIONS

At least fifty-three different sets of pieces represent solutions. They are shown in the figure on pages 87–90. Can you find one that is not on the list? If so, let us know. (E-mail any new solution to baggett@nmsu.edu.)

## A SECOND FOLLOW-UP

Students get the list of solutions and five 5 by 8 index cards of different colors, and a paper clip or an envelope. They choose any five solutions from the list, design the patterns on the index cards, and cut them out. They take their "puzzles" home.

## A LIST OF SOLUTIONS

The numbers printed under the solutions in the figure on pages 87–90 have the following meaning:

- In the first row, the first three numbers are the numbers of one-inch squares in each of the three pieces forming the $3 \times 3$ square. The fourth number is 16.

- In the next five rows, the last three numbers are the numbers of one-inch squares in each of the three pieces forming the $4 \times 4$ square. The first number is nine.

- In the remaining six rows, the first two numbers show the sizes of parts that together form the $3 \times 3$ square, and the last two show the sizes of parts that form the $4 \times 4$ square.

Notice that several different solutions give the same numerical values.

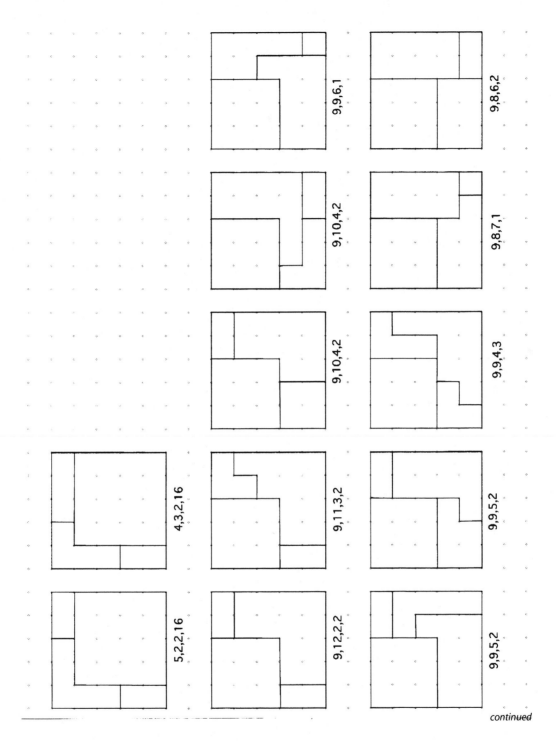

continued

*Fifty-three different sets of pieces that represent solutions.*
*See the text for the meaning of the numbers printed under each solution.*

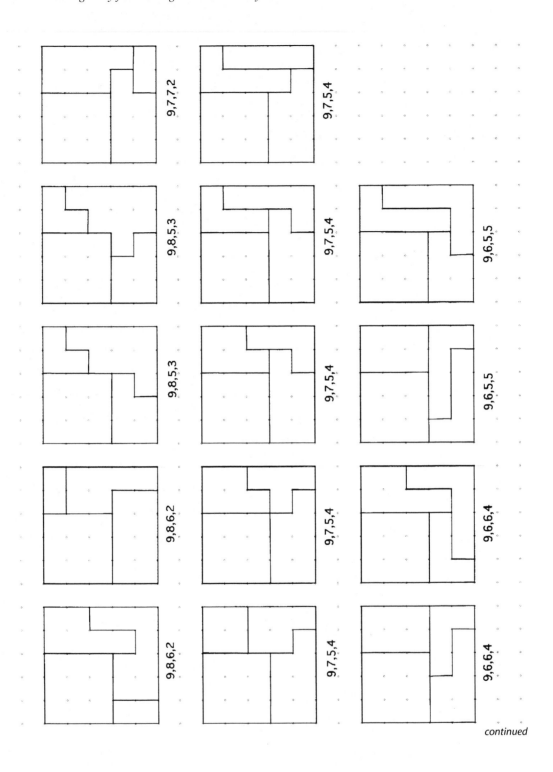

9,7,7,2

9,7,5,4

9,8,5,3

9,7,5,4

9,6,5,5

9,8,5,3

9,7,5,4

9,6,5,5

9,8,6,2

9,7,5,4

9,6,6,4

9,8,6,2

9,7,5,4

9,6,6,4

*continued*

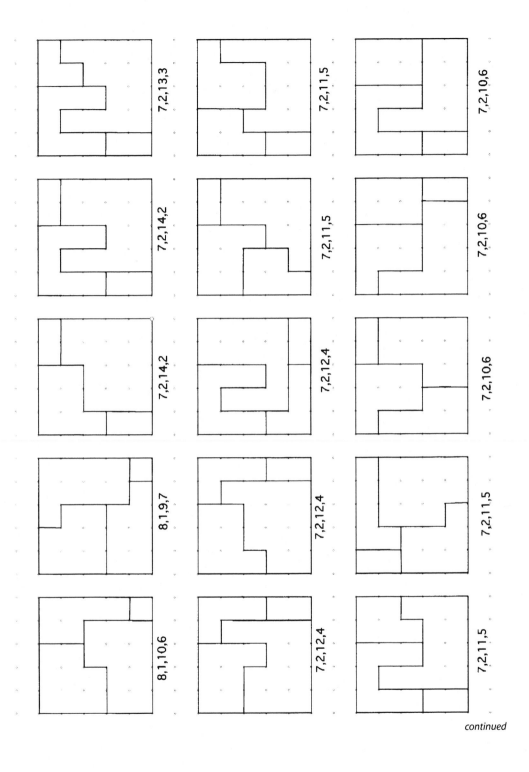

7,2,13,3

7,2,11,5

7,2,10,6

7,2,14,2

7,2,11,5

7,2,10,6

7,2,14,2

7,2,12,4

7,2,10,6

8,1,9,7

7,2,12,4

7,2,11,5

8,1,10,6

7,2,12,4

7,2,11,5

*continued*

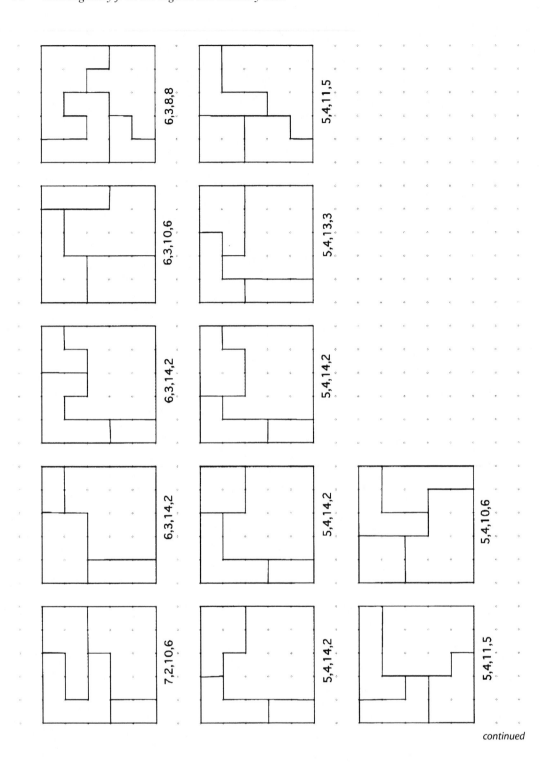

6,3,8,8

5,4,11,5

6,3,10,6

5,4,13,3

6,3,14,2

5,4,14,2

6,3,14,2

5,4,14,2

5,4,10,6

7,2,10,6

5,4,14,2

5,4,11,5

*continued*

## LESSON 33   ROAD DISTANCES AND STRAIGHT LINES

This lesson can be used in early grades and taught as an introduction to measurements with centimeters and millimeters. Children use calculators for addition and subtraction of decimals.

Each child gets a map that is a graph with 5 to 8 vertices labeled by pictures of a snail, a spider, and some insects, connected with some straight (and wide) lines.

### EXAMPLE

(See the map in the figure below with a spider, butterfly, fly, ladybug, mosquito, and snail.)

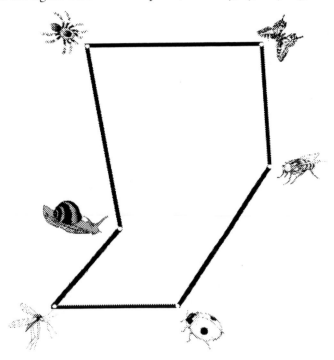

*Houses of a spider, a snail, and some insects, with roads linking them.*

### STORY

The dots on the map are houses of a spider, a snail, and some insects. The lines are roads they walk on. They cannot walk without a road because of dense grass growing everywhere. Later you may draw grass and flowers on this picture. All these animals (insects, spiders, and snails are animals) can walk, but only some of them can fly. (Which ones?) We have to find out how far they must walk to visit each other, and how far it is if they fly.

(1) Measure the lengths of the roads (segments) in centimeters and millimeters, and write the length next to each road.

(2) Children pose questions and answer them. (See also: "Ants' Roads" in *Breaking Away from the Math Book*, and "Traveling Bugs" in *Breaking Away from the Math Book II*.)

How far does the snail, who walks, have to go to visit the fly?

The snail has two ways to go. Add the lengths (using a calculator) on each path to see which way is shorter.

But if the fly visits the snail, it may fly. Who has to travel farther? How much farther?

Measure the distance between their homes, because the fly can fly straight above the grass. Find the difference between the previous value and this one. Do not forget to say the units (centimeters, or centimeters and millimeters).

(3) Color the picture!

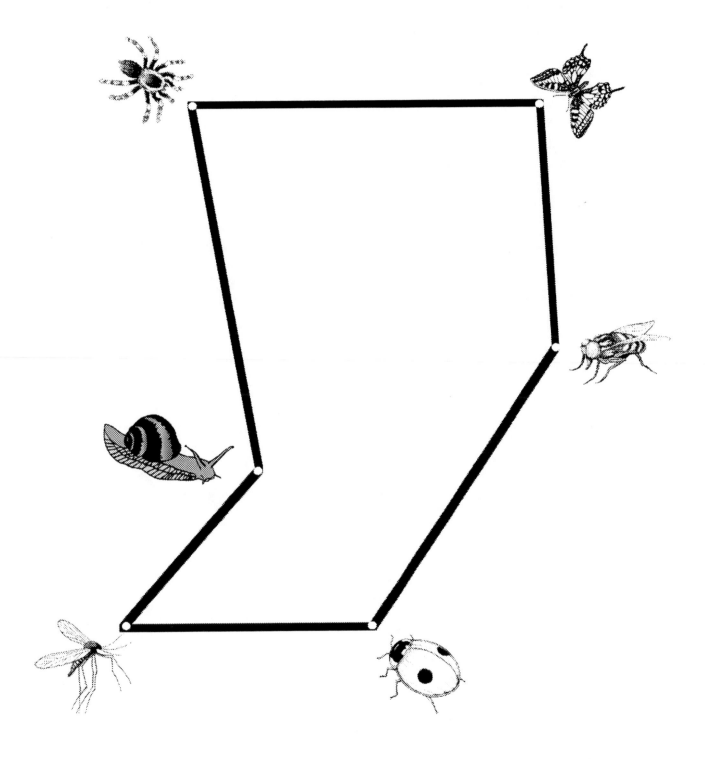

## LESSON 34  DISTANCES AND DRIVING DISTANCES IN THE SOUTHWESTERN UNITED STATES

### MATERIALS AND TOOLS

Maps of the Southwestern United States, one map for every four students. American Automobile Association (AAA) maps are excellent. We were able to obtain a classroom set free. They have a scale of 1 : 2,535,000 and include a small schematic map of driving distances; rulers with an accuracy of ¹⁄₁₆ inch; and calculators.

On a road map, roads are often shown as curvy lines. But distances "as the crow flies" are straight lines. We will compare road distances (driving distances) and distances "as the crow flies."

### TASK

On the small inset map (see figure on facing page), driving distances between different cities are listed. Students divide the work among themselves, with each student (or a small group) handling a few distances.

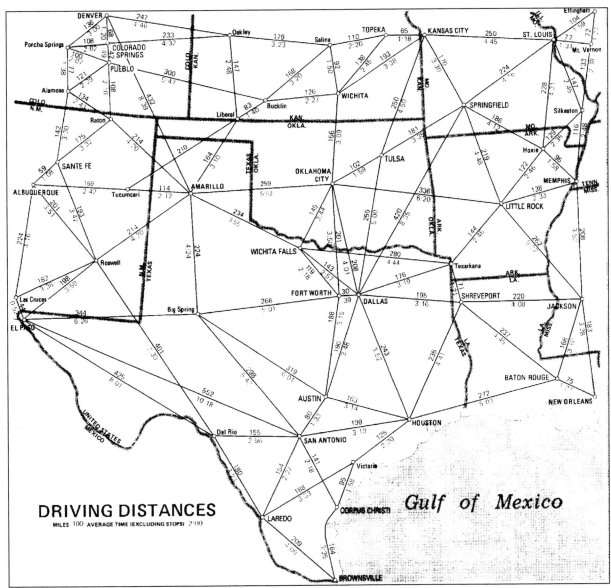

*Driving distances in the Southwestern United States.*

For example, Jill's assignment is Austin to Big Spring, Austin to Fort Worth, and Big Spring to Fort Worth. She has to make a data sheet that includes driving distances between these cities read from the map, distances "as the crow flies" (along straight lines), which she must measure and compute, and their ratios. Her finished sheet may look like that shown in the table below.

PREPARED BY JILL

| Towns: | Driving distance, D | Straight line distance, S | Ratio D/S |
|---|---|---|---|
| Austin to Big Spring | 319 mi. | 260 mi. | 1.23 |
| Austin to Fort Worth | 188 mi. | 170 mi. | 1.11 |
| Big Spring to Fort Worth | 266 mi. | 245 mi. | 1.09 |

## STEPS REQUIRED

First we have to know how many miles are represented by one inch on the map in the figure on the facing page. We read that it is approximately 40. We can check the accuracy of this approximation. A scale of 1:2,535,000 means that 1 inch on the map represents 2,535,000 inches on earth. Inches per mile is calculated as 5,280 feet per mile times 12 inches per foot: 5,280*12 = 63,360 inches per mile. Thus, 1 inch on the map represents 2,535,000/63,360 = 40.0094569 miles on earth. So 40 miles is a close approximation.

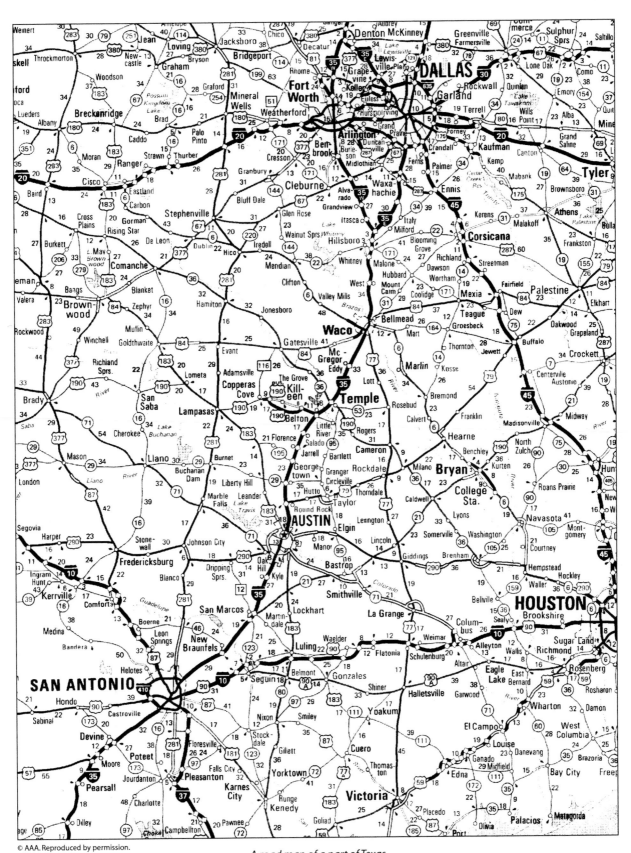

*A road map of a part of Texas.*

Next we measure distances on the map in the figure above with an accuracy of $\frac{1}{16}$ inch and multiply them by 40 to get the distances on earth measured in miles. (Note that maps are not identical. So the distances in inches on the map that you use may be slightly different from the distances in inches that we measured on our map.)

Follow the preparation of the data with a class discussion. This discussion might include the observation that driving distance cannot be shorter than the distance measured along a straight line. A helpful discussion will also cover scale and the topic of map making. Finally, students could propose some possible explanations about why the ratios *D/S* vary as much as they do.

## LESSON 35   GEOMETRIC SURPRISE

(1) Draw four straight lines intersecting in one point *P*, forming eight equal angles, each measuring 45 degrees. Choose a point *C* on one line as a center, and draw a circle around it that passes through *P*. This circle has four points of intersection with the lines. Connect these points. What figure do they form? (See the figure below.)

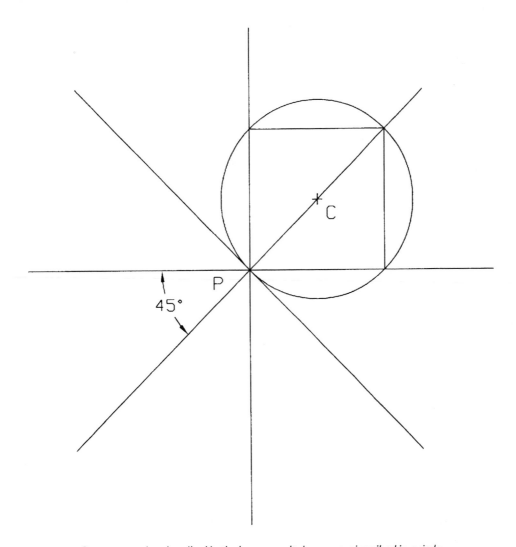

*One construction described in the lesson results in a square inscribed in a circle.*

(2) Draw six straight lines intersecting in one point *P*, forming 12 equal angles, each measuring 30 degrees. Choose a point *C* on one line as a center, and draw a circle around it that passes through *P*. This circle has six points of intersection with the lines. Connect these points. What figure do they form? (See the figure below.)

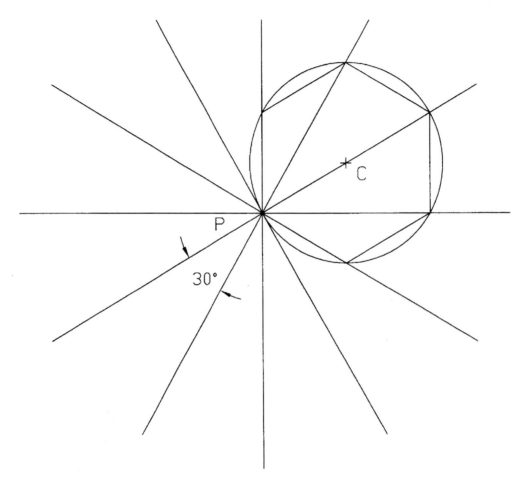

*The second construction in the lesson results in a regular hexagon inscribed in a circle.*

What do you think happens? Why?

## ANSWERS

You get a square and a regular hexagon, because any two triangles inscribed in a circle that have equal angles next to their apex (the vertex opposite the base), also have equal bases.

## LESSON 36   PENTAGON INSCRIBED IN A CIRCLE

### TOOLS

Compass, ruler, protractor, TI-30X IIS calculator

### TASK 1

Draw a regular pentagon inscribed in a circle. Compute its area as a percentage of the area of the circle.

### SOLUTION

(1) Divide the circle into five equal parts using a protractor, and draw the pentagon.

(2) Name the length of the radius of your circle $R$. You do not have to measure it. Observe that the pentagon consists of 10 right triangles, each having a hypotenuse of length $R$, and one of the angles measuring $A = 360/10 = 36$ degrees. (See the figure below.)

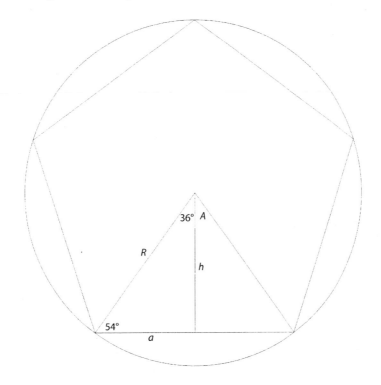

*A regular pentagon inscribed in a circle covers 75.7 percent of the area of the circle.*

(3) Area of small right triangle = $1/2*a*b$.

$$\sin A = a/R$$

$$\cos A = b/R$$

$$a = R*\sin A$$

$$b = R*\cos A$$

So:

area of small right triangle = $1/2*R*\sin A*R*\cos A = (R^2*\sin A*\cos A)/2$

Thus the area of the pentagon is $5*R^2*\sin A*\cos A$.

(4) The area of the circle is $\pi*R^2$.

(5) The ratio of the area of the pentagon to the area of the circle is

$(5*R^2*\sin A*\cos A)/(\pi*R^2) = 5*\sin A*\cos A/\pi$,

and it has to be written as a percentage.

(6) The keystrokes are:

[5][SIN][36][)][×][COS][36][)][/][$\pi$][2nd][%][=]

and they return 75.68267286.

## ANSWER

The area of a regular pentagon inscribed in a circle is approximately 75.7 percent of the area of the circle.

## TASK 2

Draw any regular *n*-gon inscribed in a circle. Compute its area as a percentage of the area of the circle.

## SOLUTION

(1) Divide the circle into *n* equal parts using a protractor, and draw the *n*-gon. As in the previous task, observe that the *n*-gon consists of 2\**n* right triangles, each having a hypotenuse of length *R*, and one of the angles measuring $A = 360/(2*n) = 180/n$ degrees.

(2) The ratio of the area of the inscribed *n*-gon to the area of the circle is

$$[n*\sin(180/n)*\cos(180/n)]/\pi$$

(3) The keystrokes are:

[*n*][SIN][180][/][*n*][)][×][COS][180][/][*n*][)][/][π][2nd][% ][=]

The following table shows some values.

| Regular polygon with *n* sides | Percentage of area of circle that is covered |
|:---:|:---:|
| 3 | 41.35% |
| 4 | 63.66% |
| 5 | 75.7% |
| 18 | 97.98% |
| 48 | 99.71% |
| 100 | 99.93 |
| 1000 | 99.999% |

# Three-Dimensional Geometry

## LESSON 37  PUFFY STARS

*Figure A. A star with five rays*

*Figure B. A stubby star with seven rays*

*Figure C. A skinny star with seven rays*

### TOOLS AND SUPPLIES

Poster board, compass, protractor, ruler, scissors, Scotch tape, and cotton balls

### ACTIVITY

Make two congruent flat stars with *n* identical rays. Each flat star is made of 2\**n* triangles that meet at the center of the star. (See the patterns in figures D and E. Figure D makes a star with five rays, and figure E makes a stubby star with seven rays.)

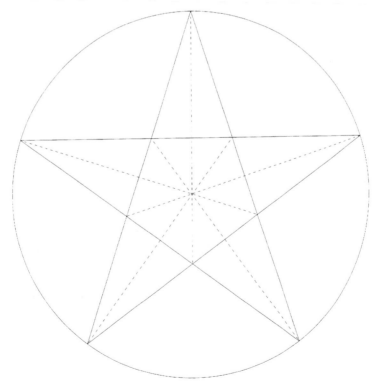

*Figure D. Pattern for a five-pointed star*

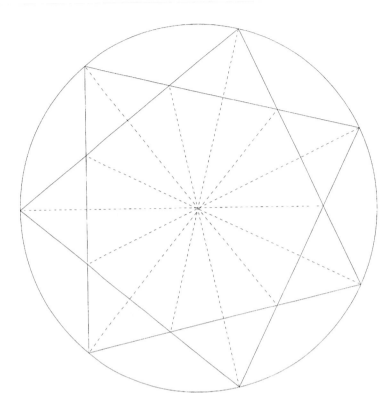

*Figure E. Pattern for a stubby seven-pointed star*

All the triangles are joined by "hinges." Our preferred method for obtaining this effect is to make the stars from one piece of poster board, scoring the lines between the triangles (the dotted lines in figures D and E), and creasing along the scored lines. Another way to do it is to cut separate triangles from poster board or index cards and then to join them with transparent tape.

Join both stars along their border with transparent tape. Before you close the pocket, you may stuff a few cotton balls inside to make the star three-dimensional. Now tape the pocket closed.

If you leave the cotton out, then when you squeeze the star sideways, it becomes three-dimensional.

You may punch a hole through a tip and string the star with yarn to make a decoration!

By choosing the number of rays, 3, 4, 5, 6, . . . , and by choosing their shapes from stubby to skinny, you may create a variety of stars. Stars with five and seven rays are shown in figures A through C. Two seven-ray stars are shown, a stubby one and a skinny one.

The underlying principle is simple. You build two pyramids with stellar (star-shaped) bases, and you join them at their bases.

## LESSON 38 SKELETAL POLYHEDRA

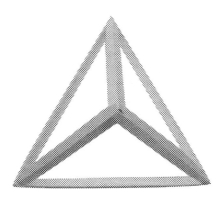

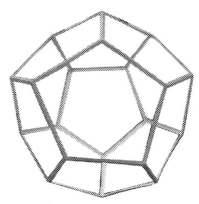

*A skeletal tetrahedron with six ribs*

*A skeletal dodecahedron with 30 ribs*

The task is to construct several large skeletons of polyhedra that you can use later in geometry and art lessons.

The simplest skeletal polyhedron, the tetrahedron (see figure above left), can be made by second and third graders. The dodecahedal skeleton (see figure above right) is a challenge to make in middle school. Polyhedra with faces of different shapes are especially challenging, because the ends of the ribs are tricky to design.

### MATERIALS

Poster board, preferably colored on one side and white on the other, and glue (We have found that wood glue or glue guns work best.)

### TOOLS

Rulers (meter sticks are helpful), protractors, good scissors, a table knife or fingernail file or point of a compass for making a straight-line groove in the poster board before creasing, 3-inch by 5-inch index card for making a tool for the ends of the ribs, with stapler and paper cutter optional

### GENERAL DESCRIPTION

- For a given polyhedron, each edge (or rib) is constructed as a V-shaped straight piece of poster board. The preferred width of each side of the V, \ and /, of the edge is 1 cm, (between 0.5 and 1.5 cm). (If a stapler is used, we recommend ½ inch rather than 1 cm.) Thus, the two sides of the V-shaped rib lie on two adjacent faces of the polyhedron. The straight line down the center of the rib should have the exact length of the intended edge.

- The ribs meeting at one vertex must be glued (or glued and stapled) together. This requires very precise tapering of the ends.

## EXAMPLE

Let's try to make a rib *AB* sitting between a rectangular face and a triangular face. (See the figure below.)

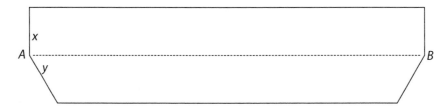

*A rib that connects a rectangular face and a triangular face of a polyhedron*

The angles *x* and *y* at the *A* end of the rib MUST be equal to the angles *x* and *y* on the corners of two faces of the polyhedron.

## MAKING A TOOL

Let's make a tool for tracing the ends of ribs for deltahedra. (Regular deltahedra are convex polyhedra with equilateral triangles for faces.) The tool's design is shown in the figure below. It is made from a 3-inch by 5-inch index card, and it has a tip that measures 120°, or 60° on each side.

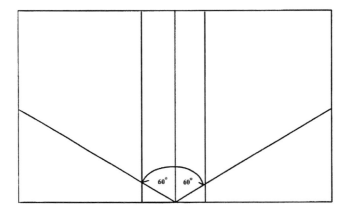

*Designing a tool for ribs of polyhedra with equilateral triangles for faces*

To make the tool, find the midpoints of the 5-inch sides of the card, and draw a line connecting them. Using a protractor, mark 60° angles as shown. Decide how wide you want your ribs to be, and draw lines one-half of the desired width on each side of the center line. (A width of one inch is shown in the figure above.) Very carefully cut out the tool.

## MAKING RIBS FOR DELTAHEDRA

A tetrahedron requires six ribs. One plan for the ribs is shown in figure A. (Use the tool you have made to trace both ends of the rib.) An octahedron (figure B) requires twelve ribs. A deltahedron with 16 faces (figure C) requires 24 ribs. An icosahedron (figure D) requires 30 ribs.

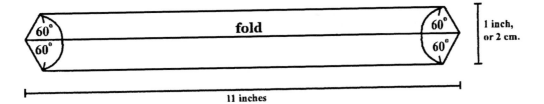

*Figure A. A rib for a tetrahedron or any deltahedron*

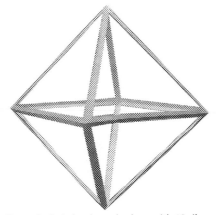

*Figure B. A skeletal octahedron with 12 ribs*

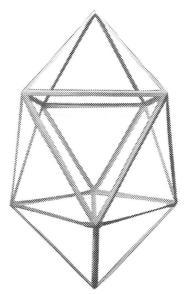

*Figure C. A deltahedron with 24 ribs*

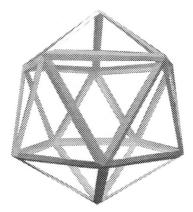

*Figure D. An icosahedron with 30 ribs*

The ribs may be up to 3 feet long and the polyhedron will still be rigid enough to keep its shape.

Making a straight pressed-in groove in the middle of the edge before bending it into a V-shape is essential! It determines the straightness of the edge. So score the rib before you cut it. (You may cut it with a paper cutter.)

## PLANNING A TASK

This task is time consuming. The best way is to distribute the task among small groups of students, with each group making only a few ribs and then collaborating with other groups during the assembly (gluing) phase. (One skilled person may spend about 2 hours making one cube or octahedron with 12 edges that are 2 feet long.) Making a tool as described in the previous section (a short rib with a correctly cut end, which you can then trace) is helpful. Gluing is tricky. A correctly glued vertex of a tetrahedron is shown schematically in figure E.

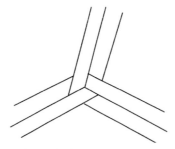

*Figure E. A schematic drawing of a correctly glued vertex of a tetrahedron*

## WHICH POLYHEDRA TO MAKE?

A tool for a dodecahedron is shown in figure F. A plan for a rib, with angles of 108°, and how it fits into the dodecahedron's skeleton, are both shown in figure G.

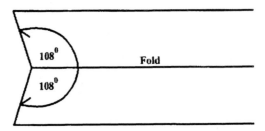

*Figure F. A tool for making the ribs of a dodecahedron*

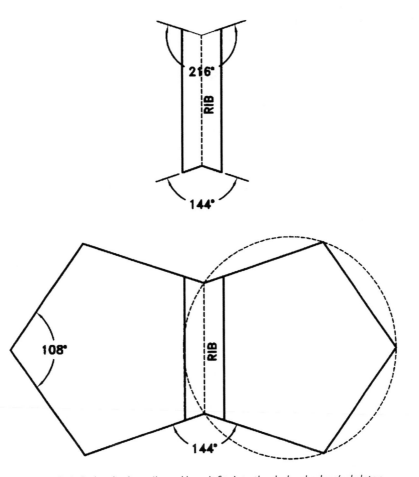

*Figure G. A dodecahedron rib, and how it fits into the dodecahedron's skeleton*

But do not restrict the task to Platonic solids. Archimedean solids, deltahedra (as in figure C, see also chapter 55, "Solids Built from Equilateral Triangles," in *Breaking Away from the Math Book II*), and irregular solids are as attractive and more unusual.

## HOW TO USE THEM

- When you make them big and colorful, they are spectacular.

- Use them in math classes for measurements of surface area and volume.

- They are useful when you talk about projections and perspective.

- They are interesting and challenging models for free-hand and technical drawings.

## LESSON 39 HOW TO DRAW AN ICOSAHEDRON

An icosahedron is a polyhedron with 20 faces, 12 vertices, and 30 edges. A regular icosahedron (an icosahedron whose faces are all equilateral triangles) is one of the five Platonic solids (tetrahedron, octahedron, cube, icosahedron, dodecahedron). Here is a simple way to draw a regular icosahedron.

(1) Draw two overlapping equilateral triangles (a Star of David) as in the figure below.

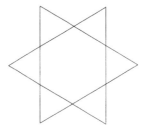

(2) From the tip of each of the six points, draw a short straight line as in the figure below.

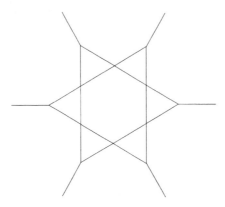

(3) Going clockwise, draw six straight lines. Each line connects the end of a short straight line drawn in step 2 to the closest tip of the star as in the figure below.

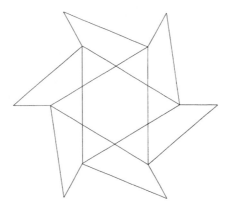

(4) Now going counterclockwise, draw six more straight lines. As in step 3, each line connects the end of a short straight line drawn in step 2 to the closest tip of the star. See the figure below.

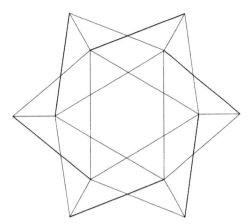

(5) Draw six more straight lines, connecting the tips of the short straight lines. You may darken them, and also darken other lines, to show the outline and the front face of the icosahedron as shown in the figure below.

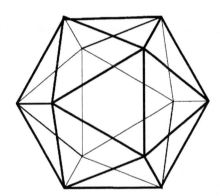

## LESSON 40    TWENTY PYRAMIDS MAKE AN ICOSAHEDRON

You may view an icosahedron as an arrangement of 20 congruent pyramids (tetrahedra) whose bases form its faces, and whose vertices meet at the icosahedron's center. As shown in the figure below, you can see one pyramid, ABCD. One vertex, D, of the pyramid, is in the center of the icosahedron, and one face, ABC, is a face of the icosahedron.

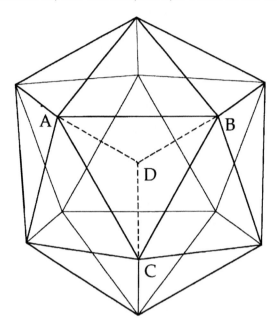

## CLASS PROJECT

Students form teams, and each team makes one or two pyramids which are later put together to form an icosahedron.

## DESIGN

In order to find the shape of these pyramids, we need to know the relationship between the length of an edge, *s*, and the length of the radius of a sphere circumscribed around the icosahedron. This information can be found on the Web and in several math books. (The actual value is

radius *r* of a circumscribed sphere = $\sqrt{(10 + 2 *\sqrt{(5)})}$ / 4 * (edge length).

The derivation of this formula (if it is presented at all) should be postponed until the task is finished.)

A good approximation that can be used is:

$r = 0.95 * s$

A reasonable size is obtained by taking *s* = 10 cm, but *s* = 20 cm is more impressive. Colored poster board is the best material.

Each pyramid has an equilateral triangle with side *s* for its base, and three isosceles triangles with sides *s*, *r*, and *r* for its sides. One plan for drawing a pyramid from scratch is shown in the following figure. Equilateral triangle ABC is its base. Note that polygon DAEBFC is not an equilateral triangle! The plan is easy to draw using Geometer's sketchpad. You may also simply Xerox the large pattern in figure A onto 20 pieces of cardstock, rather than starting from scratch.

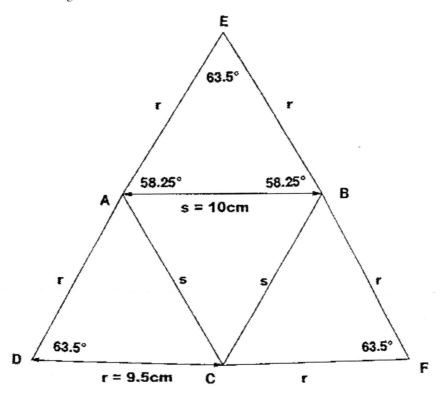

*A pattern for a pyramid (a tetrahedron)*

## ASSEMBLY

The pyramids are fastened together with transparent tape. During the final assembly, small strips of transparent tape can be used to keep the pyramids together.

## QUESTION

What percentage of the volume of a sphere with radius *r* is occupied by the iosahedron?

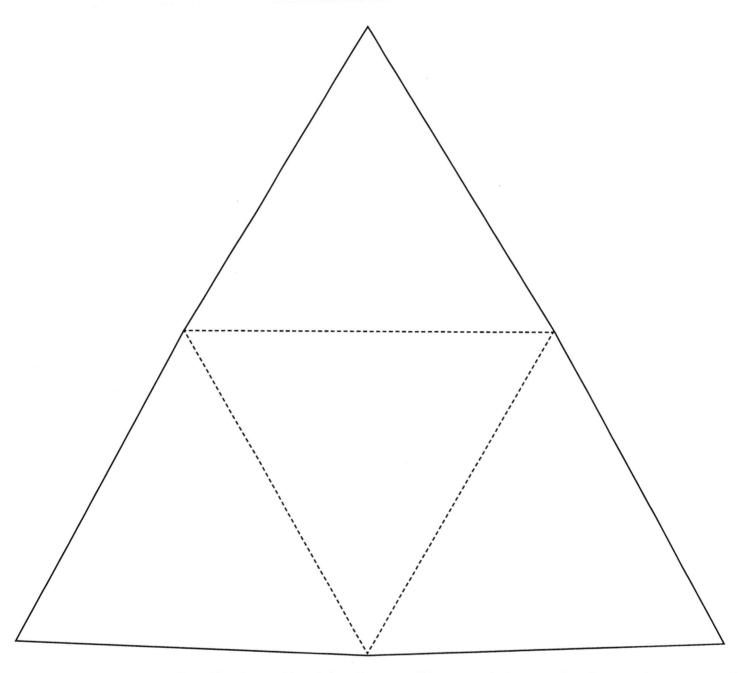

Figure A. Twenty pyramids made from this pattern will form an icosahedron. An equilateral triangle is formed by the dotted lines. Score and fold along them to make a pyramid.

## LESSON 41    FOX: A NONCONVEX POLYHEDRON

A polyhedron is a connected, three-dimensional object with no holes, which is bounded by polygons. Students in geometry classes typically build the five regular polyhedra known as the Platonic solids (tetrahedron, octahedron, cube, icosahedron, dodecahedron). Each of these polyhedra is convex, which means that any segment connecting two points within the polyhedron is inside the polyhedron.

Figure A shows the front and figure B shows the back of a nonconvex polyhedron with 10 faces. You construct the pattern for it by beginning with four congruent overlapping circles, as shown in figure C. The finished pattern is shown in figure D. After making the pattern, be sure to score along the dotted lines on the inside before folding it into the polyhedron.

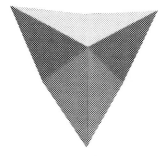

*Figure A. Front view of nonconvex poly-hedron with ten faces, called a fox*

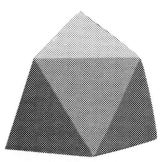

*Figure B. Back view of the fox*

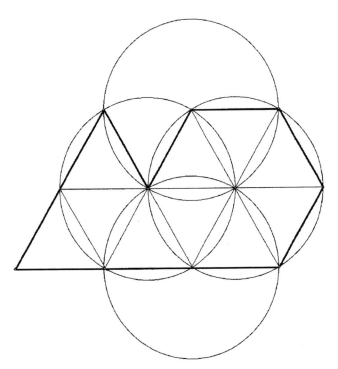

*Figure C. To draw the pattern, begin with four overlapping circles and add the straight lines as shown.*

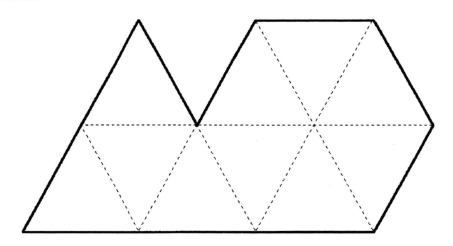

*Figure D. The complete pattern for the fox. Score along the dotted lines before folding.*

Students called the polyhedron a fox, because when you hold it right, it seems to have a narrow face and two big ears (see figure A).

## LESSON 42    TWO-PIECE TETRAHEDRON PUZZLE

A tetrahedron is a polyhedron with four triangular faces. If all the faces are equilateral triangles, the tetrahedron is called a regular tetrahedron. A tetrahedron is also a pyramid, and it is a pyramid with the smallest number of faces possible, four.

Let's make a regular tetrahedron from four equilateral triangles as shown in the figure below.) Fold along the dotted lines.

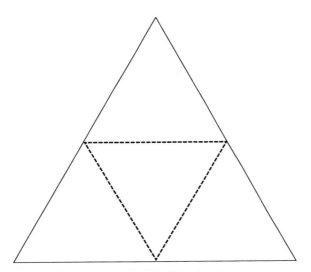

Now let's see if we can make a two-piece tetrahedron puzzle. The two pieces are congruent, and when you put their square faces together, you get a tetrahedron.

• The figure below shows a schematic diagram of how the two pieces fit together.

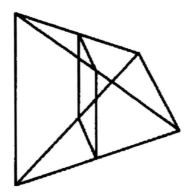

*A schematic diagram of how the two pieces of the puzzle fit together.*

- The figure below shows the two pieces, made from poster board.

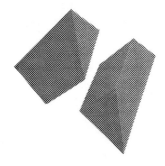

*The two pieces made from posterboard.*

- The figure below shows how they fit together.

*Turn one piece 90°, and put the two square faces together to make the tetrahedron.*

- A pattern for each of the pieces is provided in the figure below.

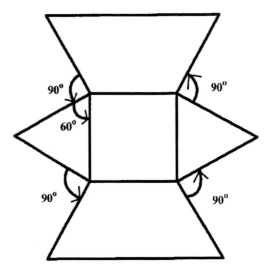

*A pattern for each of the pieces.*

- Another way to think about the pattern (with squares in each of four corners, to be cut away) is given in the figure below. It was invented by Kathy Porter, a fifth grade teacher, who taught it to her students.

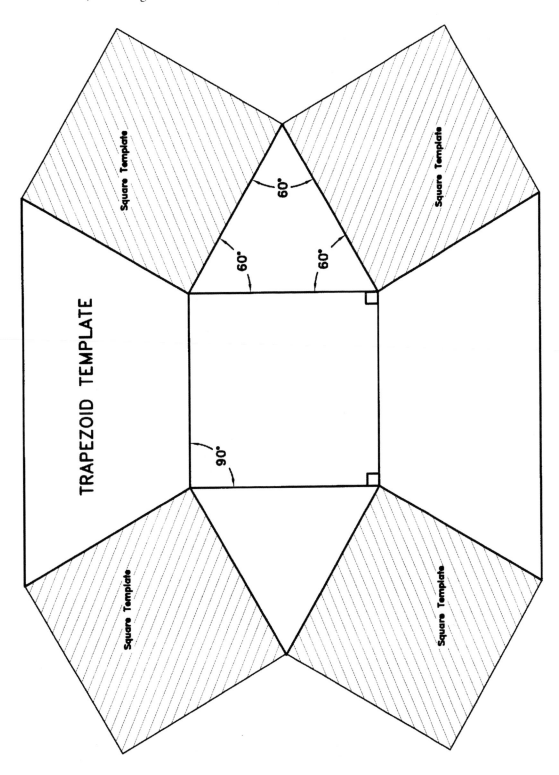

*Another way to make a pattern, invented by a fifth-grade teacher.*

## LESSON 43  FOUR-PIECE TETRAHEDRON PUZZLE I

Construct a pyramid such that:

- its base is a rhombus consisting of two equilateral triangles (with sides of length *s*);

- two of its faces are equilateral triangles (with sides of length *s*);

- two of its faces are right triangles (with legs of length *s*).

Four such pyramids can be assembled to form a regular tetrahedron (with edges of length 2*s*). The pieces make a nice puzzle. (See the figures. Figure A shows the four pyramids. Figures B and C show front and side views of the assembled tetrahedron, and figure D shows two halves of the tetrahedron.)

   A plan for the pyramid can easily be drawn with a ruler and compass (no measurements are needed).

### EXAMPLE

In this figure, ABC is a right triangle. AC = BC = *s* BDE is an equilateral triangle.

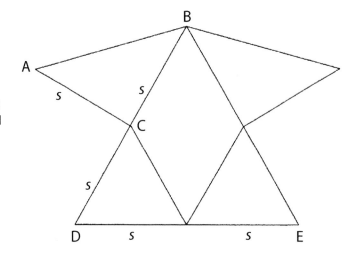

Figure A. *Four congruent pyramids that make a tetrahedron.*

Figure B. *A front view of the assembled tetrahedron.*

Figure C. A different view of
the tetrahedron.

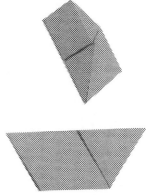

Figure D. Two halves of the tetrahedron,
each made with two pyramids.

(1) Discuss different plans for making this pyramid.

(2) Compute its surface area.

(3) Compute its volume.

## ANSWERS

Height of equilateral triangle BDE = $\sqrt{((2{*}s)^2 - s^2)}$ = $\sqrt{(4{*}s^2 - s^2)}$ = $\sqrt{3}{*}s$

Area of equilateral triangle = $2{*}s{*}\sqrt{3}\,{*}s/2$ = $\sqrt{3}\,{*}s^2$

Area of right triangle ABC = $s^2/2$

Total surface area of pyramid (including base) = $(1 + \sqrt{3}\,){*}s^2$.

Compute the volume of the big tetrahedron (see lesson 45 in this book entitled "A Cube and a Tetrahedron with the Same Volume") and divide it by 4 to get the volume of one pyramid.

## LESSON 44    FOUR-PIECE TETRAHEDRON PUZZLE II

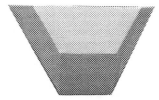

*A truncated pyramid. Four of these can be assembled to make a regular tetrahedron.*

This puzzle consists of four congruent (same shape, same size) truncated pyramids (pyramids with their tops cut off as in the figure above). They can be put together to form a regular tetrahedron as shown in the figure below. Each truncated pyramid has six faces, but not all the faces are congruent. One face is a square, and the other five are trapezoids. Three different sizes of trapezoids are used.

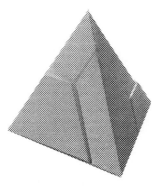

*A regular tetrahedron consisting of four truncated pyramids.*

Students can make by hand the pattern for each truncated pyramid, following the drawing that shows angles and edge lengths (see figure below). One inch is a nice length for *a*. They can also draw the pattern using Geometer's Sketchpad or some other drawing program. The four patterns in the figure on the following page may be photocopied onto card stock.

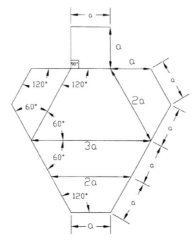

*A pattern for a truncated pyramid.*

*You may photocopy this page onto cardstock and make the four truncated pyramids.*

After cutting out the patterns, score along the dotted lines with the point of a compass or other sharp object to help you make crisp folds. Now fasten the faces together with transparent tape.

Arranging the four truncated pyramids into a tetrahedron is tricky. A side-view diagram of the finished product is shown below.

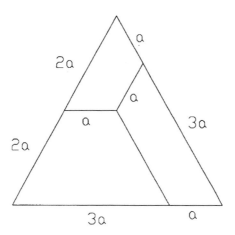

*A side-view diagram of the finished tetrahedron showing the pieces.*

## VARIATION OF THIS LESSON

In an advanced class we made the truncated pyramids as skeletal polyhedra, and we formed a four-piece skeletal tetrahedron!

## LESSON 45   A CUBE AND A TETRAHEDRON WITH THE SAME VOLUME

### TASK

Construct a cube and a regular tetrahedron, each with a volume of 1 cubic inch, like those shown in the figure below.

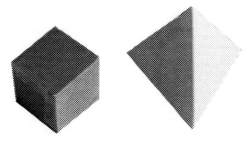

*The cube and the tetrahedron have the same volume.*

### COMMENT

This lesson can be taught on different levels, depending on whether the formula for the volume is given or derived, and whether the algorithm for the cube root is given or derived.

In Part 1 of this unit we give the formula and the algorithm, and children simply compare two solids with the same volume but different shapes. In Part 2 we derive the formula for the volume of a tetrahedron.

### Part 1

### Cube

The volume V of a cube with edge *s* is discussed:

$$V = s^3$$

where $V$ is measured in cubic inches and $s$ is measured in inches.

Children make a cube with a volume of 1 cubic inch from colored construction paper or cardstock. They should leave one flap open so that it can be filled with rice.

### Regular Tetrahedron

The volume $V$ of a regular tetrahedron with edge *s* is:

$$V = s^3/(6*\sqrt{2})$$

Thus:

$$s = \sqrt[3]{V * 6 * \sqrt{2}}.$$

So for $V = 1$ cu. in.,

$$s = \sqrt[3]{6 * \sqrt{2}}.$$

Here is an algorithm for the cube root of $z$, where $z = 6 * \sqrt{2}$:

$$s := \sqrt{z}$$

Repeat: $s := \sqrt{(z * s)}$

($s :=$ means "assign to $s$")

This program for the cube root of $z$ can be executed on the TI-108 calculator:

$$[z][*][\sqrt{\ }]$$

Repeat: $[=][\sqrt{\ }][\sqrt{\ }]$

(See also http://math.nmsu.edu/breakingaway/Lessons/chinesebox1/chinesebox.html.)

The following program transforms a decimal into a mixed number that is rounded to the nearest sixteenth of an inch. Let $w$ be the whole part of the number on the display.

$$[-][w][*][16][=]$$

Round the display to a whole number $p$. The answer is $w + p/16$.

Computation of side length $s$:

| Keystrokes: | Display: | Comments: |
|---|---|---|
| $[2][\sqrt{\ }][*][6][*][\sqrt{\ }]$ | 2.9129505 | This is the initial value of $s$, which equals $\sqrt{z}$ |
| $[=][\sqrt{\ }][\sqrt{\ }]$ | 2.2297174 | |
| $[=][\sqrt{\ }][\sqrt{\ }]$ | 2.0855903 | |
| $[=][\sqrt{\ }][\sqrt{\ }]$ | 2.0510384 | |
| $[=][\sqrt{\ }][\sqrt{\ }]$ | 2.0424902 | |
| $[=][\sqrt{\ }][\sqrt{\ }]$ | 2.0403588 | |
| $[=][\sqrt{\ }][\sqrt{\ }]$ | 2.0398262 | good enough, $w = 2$ |
| $[-][2][*][16][=]$ | 0.6372192 | $p = 1$ ($p = 0$ is also acceptable) |

Answer: $s = 2\frac{1}{16}$ inches

Now children draw a plan, cut it out, and make a tetrahedron. They may leave one flap open and fill the tetrahedron with rice, and then pour the rice into the cubic inch they made previously. They will be surprised that it fits exactly!

## Part 2

Deriving the formula for the volume of a regular tetrahedron. (See the figure below.)

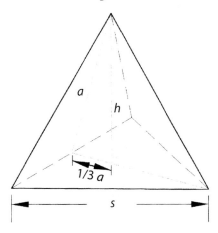

*The height of a tetrahedron can be found using the Pythagorean theorem.*

Let:

     *s*    be the length of a side
     *h*    be the height
     *a*    be the slant height

Then:

$$h^2 + (\frac{1}{3}a)^2 = a^2$$

$$h^2 = a^2(1 - \frac{1}{9})$$

$$h^2 = \frac{8}{9}a^2$$

$$h = \sqrt{\frac{8}{9}} * a$$

Looking now at one face of the tetrahedron (see figure below):

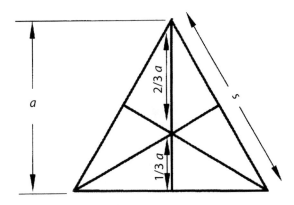

*The height of the triangle can be found using the Pythagorean theorem.*

$$(\frac{s}{2})^2 + a^2 = s^2$$

$$a^2 = s^2 * \frac{3}{4}$$

$$a = \sqrt{\frac{3}{4}} * s$$

$$b = \sqrt{\frac{8}{9}} * a = \sqrt{\frac{8}{9}} * \sqrt{\frac{3}{4}} * s = \sqrt{\frac{8*3}{9*4}} * s = \sqrt{\frac{2}{3}} * s$$

$$\text{area of base} = \frac{s}{2} * a$$

$$= \frac{s}{2} * \sqrt{\frac{3}{4}} * s = \frac{\sqrt{\frac{3}{4}}}{2} * s^3$$

$$\text{volume} = \text{area of base} * \frac{b}{3} = \frac{\sqrt{\frac{3}{4}}}{2} * s^2 * \frac{\sqrt{\frac{2}{3}}}{3} * s$$

$$= \frac{\sqrt{\frac{3*2}{4*3}}}{6} * s^3$$

$$= \frac{\sqrt{\frac{1}{2}}}{6} s^3 = \frac{1}{6\sqrt{2}} * s^3$$

If volume = 1 cubic inch, then:

$$1 = \frac{1}{6\sqrt{2}} * s^3, \text{ and}$$

$$s^3 = 6\sqrt{2}, \text{ so}$$

$$s = \sqrt[3]{6\sqrt{2}} \approx 2.04 \text{ inches.}$$

So the edge length of a regular tetrahedron with a volume of 1 cubic inch is approximately 2.04 inches.

## LESSON 46   TWO CYLINDERS

### MATERIALS AND TOOLS

Index cards, 3 inches by 5 inches (three cards per person), Scotch tape, compasses, good scissors, calculators, and pennies

### TASK 1

Make two cylinders from index cards, one 3 inches tall, and the other 5 inches tall, and slender. Fasten them together carefully from the inside and outside with Scotch tape so the surface of the side area is, in both cases, 15 sq. inches. Provide them with tightly fitting circular bottoms, also fastened with Scotch tape. Put a few pennies inside and they will stand up straight.

### REMARKS

- Don't expect that children will succeed in making the cylinders on the first attempt.

- Making the shorter container is much easier than making the taller one.

- Before using Scotch tape, gently roll the card into a cylinder between your palms.

- Use two long strips of tape (1 inside, 1 outside) to fasten together the side of each cylinder.

- How to design the bottoms of the cylinders? Call the circumference of a cylinder $c$, the diameter of its base $d$, and the radius of its base $r$. Then $c = \pi * d = 2 * \pi * r$, where $\pi \approx 3.14$. For the short cylinder, $c = 5$ inches, and for the tall cylinder, $c = 3$ inches. So, for the short cylinder, $2 * \pi * r = 5$, and $r = 5/(2 * \pi) \approx 0.8$ inches $\approx 12.7/16$ inches. Construct a circle with approximately this radius for the bottom. For the tall cylinder, $2 * \pi * r = 3$, and $r = 3/(2 * \pi) \approx 0.48$ inches $\approx 7.5/16$ inches. Construct a circle with approximately this radius for the bottom.

- Put two or three strips of tape crosswise to attach each circle to the bottom. It is better if the strips are very narrow. (You can cut the tape in half lengthwise.)

### TASK 2

Have children estimate the relative volumes of the two cylinders. Do they have the same volume? If not, which one has greater volume, and how much greater? (When we have posed this question in college courses, the overwhelming vote is that the cylinders have the same volume!)

Now compute the volumes of both cylinders. (For young learners you may prefer to fill the two cylinders with rice, rather than actually computing the volume.)

## SOLUTION

Let:

| | |
|---|---|
| $V$ | be the volume of the cylinder |
| $h$ | be its height |
| $B$ | be the area of its base |
| $r$ | be the radius of the base |

Relations among variables:

$B = \pi * r^2$, and $V = B*h$, and therefore
$V = \pi * r^2 * h$

For the short cylinder:

$r = 5/(2*\pi)$, and $h = 3$, and therefore
$V = \pi*(5/(2\pi))^2*3 = 75/(4\pi) \approx 6$ cu. in.

For the tall cylinder:

$r = 3/(2*\pi)$, and $h = 5$, and therefore
$V = \pi*(3/(2\pi))^2*5 = 45/(4\pi) \approx 3.6$ cu. in.

The ratio of the volume of the short cylinder to the volume of the tall one is $(75/(4\pi))/(45/(4\pi)) = 75/45 = 5/3 = 1\ 2/3$. So the short cylinder is two-thirds ($\approx 67\%$) bigger than the tall one. (The ratio of the volumes is exactly the ratio of the height of the tall cylinder to the height of the short cylinder. In general, when two cylinders are made from rectangular cards with dimensions $x$ and $y$, the ratio of their volumes is $y/x$.)

You can show how the volumes compare by filling the cylinders with rice. It will take $1\frac{2}{3}$ fillings of the tall cylinder to fill the short one once, or five tall cylinders to fill three short ones. (See the figure below.)

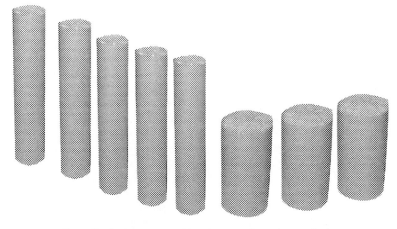

*Five tall cylinders are equal in volume to three short cylinders.*

## LESSON 47   CONE

Description of a cone as shown in the figure below:

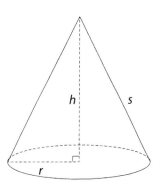

Variables:

| | |
|---|---|
| $h$ | height |
| $r$ | radius of the base |
| $s$ | length of the slope (also called slant height) |
| $V$ | volume of the cone |

Relationships among the variables:

$$h^2 + r^2 = s^2$$
$$B = \pi {}^* r^2$$
$$V = B {}^* h / 3$$

where $\pi = 3.14159 \ldots$

## TASK

- From an index card, 5 inches by 8 inches, make a cone (with a base) that has the length of its slope $s = 2.5$ inches, and the radius of its base $r = (3/4)^* s$ (three-quarters of the length of its slope).

- Compute its height, the area of its base, and its volume.

- Draw its side view and top view on a sheet of paper with a scale of 1 : 2.

(You may use a TI-108 calculator.)

## DESIGN

We have to cut out a circular base with radius

$$r = 3/4 {}^* 2.5 = 1.875 = 1\tfrac{7}{8} \text{ in.,}$$

and a sector of *A* degrees of a circle with a radius *s* = 2.5 inches, for the side of the cone. But what is *A*?

A/360 of the perimeter of the big circle is the perimeter of the base.

Thus

$(A/360)*2* \pi *s = 2* \pi *r.$

And therefore

$A = 360*r/s = 360*3/4 = 270$ degrees.

We cannot draw the two whole circles on one index card without overlap, but we can draw 3/4 of the big circle and the whole smaller circle (see figure below).

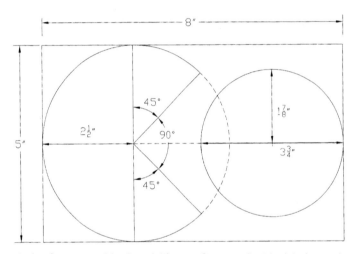

*A plan for a cone with a base laid out to fit on a 5- by 8-inch index card.*

Students finish the task by:

- making the cone (attaching the base to the side with Scotch tape is rather tricky);
- computing the height, the area of the base, and the volume; and
- drawing two views of the cone with a scale of 1 : 2 (check the drawings for correctness).

## LESSON 48   CLAY BALLS

*Electronic scales are used to weigh a clay ball with
an accuracy of one gram. The ball weighs 62 grams.*

In this lesson we used Extra Measures electronic scales, which have an accuracy of 1 gram. (See the figure above.) We also used TI-108 calculators.

### MATERIALS AND TOOLS

Scales (one for each group of three children), Play-Doh® or other clay, and calculators

For many substances, such as clay, volume is proportional to weight. Therefore many problems that are formulated in terms of volumes can be solved by weighing.

Children work in groups of three. Each group gets one set of scales, and one can of Play-Doh or other clay.

### PRELIMINARY TASKS

(We tried these activities in second grade.)

(1) How much does your clay weigh?

Procedure.

- Weigh the entire lump of clay. Record its total weight $t$ in grams.

(2) Using all your clay, make two balls, each with the same volume, which means they should weigh the same.

Procedure.

- Divide the weight of your clay by 2:

    $[t][\div][2][=]$

- Divide the clay into two lumps, weighing each one and adjusting the amounts until both weigh the required amount.

(3) Again, using all your clay, make three balls, each with the same volume.

Procedure.

- Divide the weight of your clay by 3:

    [*t*][÷][3][=]

- Divide the clay into three lumps, weighing each one and adjusting the amounts until all three weigh the required amount.

## MAIN TASK

Using all the clay, make three balls whose volumes are in the ratio of 1 to 2 to 3. (This task is more advanced.)

## SOLUTION

Because volumes are proportional to weights, divide the clay into three lumps with weights having ratios 1 to 2 to 3. Then roll each lump into a ball (see figure below).

*Three clay balls whose weights are in the ratio 1:2:3.*

- As before, weigh the whole clay and record its total weight *t* in grams.

- Compute 1/6\**t*, 2/6\**t*, 3/6\**t*, and you have the weight of three lumps.

- Divide the clay into three lumps, weighing each one and adjusting the amount until the target weights are achieved.

The total weight *t* of our clay was 185.5 grams.

Calculation:

    [185.5][/][6][=]   30.916666
    [*][2][=]          61.833332
    [3][=]             92.749998

So the target weights were 31 g, 62 g, and 93 g.

We were able to achieve all three target weights. (Remember that our scales have an accuracy of 1 g. We recorded 185.5 because the scales oscillated between 185 g and 186 g.)

## REMARKS

This method is a general one. Suppose you want to divide your clay into $k$ balls whose volumes are in the ratios $a_1 : a_2 : a_3 : \ldots : a_k$. Let $A = a_1 + a_2 + a_3 + \ldots + a_k$, and let $t$ be the total weight of the balls. Form $k$ balls, weighing $(a_1/A)^*t$, $(a_2/A)^*t$, $\ldots$, $(a_k/A)^*t$.

## LESSON 49   HOW WELL DO YOU KNOW A CUBE?

Imagine a cube 1 foot by 1 foot by 1 foot, built from cubic inches (small cubes 1 inch by 1 inch by 1 inch).

### QUESTIONS

(1) How many cubes are on the surface? How many are inside?

(2) What are the general formulas? (Assume that the edge of the cube is a whole number of inches.)

### REMARKS

Try this problem as a problem in "mental geometry." Many students will need a model of a cube and/or some drawings, however, in order to understand the formulas. We have also made cubic inch blocks available to students, so they can build 2 by 2 by 2 cubic inch cubes, 3 by 3 by 3 cubic inch cubes, etc. At least one concrete computation should be made before the second question is answered.

### ONE WAY TO ANSWER THE FIRST QUESTION

A foot has 12 inches. So the cube contains 12*12*12 = 1728 cu. in. (See the figure below.)

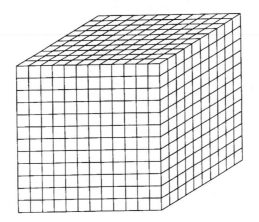

| Parts of surface: | Small cubes: |
|---|---|
| 8 corners (see figure below): | 8 |
| 12 edges, each with 10 cubes (not counting corners): | 12*10 = 120 |
| 6 faces, each with 10*10 = 100 cubes (not counting edges): | 6*100 = 600 |

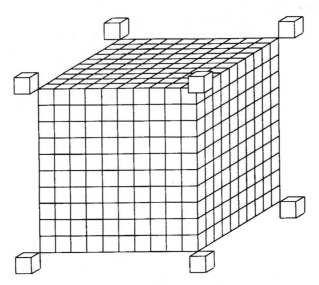

*The cube has 8 corners (one is not shown!).*

The following figure shows edges with 10 cubes and faces with 100 cubes.

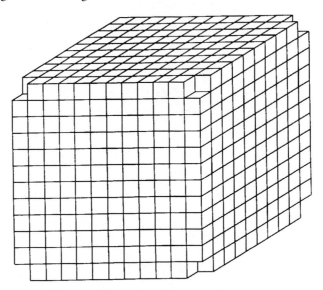

*The large cube without its corners, showing edges with 10 small cubes and faces with 100 small cubes.*

Thus we have 8 + 120 + 600 = 728 small cubes on the surface, and 1728 − 728 = 1000 small cubes inside. (See the following figure, showing the inside.)

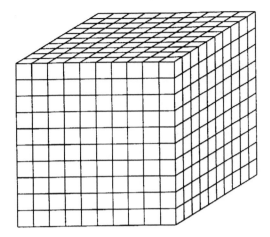

If we take off one layer of surface, we are left with 1728 – 728 = 1000 small cubes inside.

## WAYS TO ANSWER THE SECOND QUESTION USING DIFFERENT FORMULAS

Let $n$ be length of the edge in inches. So the whole cube contains $n^3$ small cubes. Let SUR be the number of small cubes on the surface and INS the number of small cubes inside.

(1) General version of the solution already given.

| Parts of surface: | Small cubes: |
|---|---|
| 8 corners: | 8 |
| 12 edges, each with $n – 2$ cubes (not counting corners): | $12*(n – 2)$ |
| 6 faces, each with $(n – 2)^2$ cubes (not counting edges): | $6*(n – 2)^2$ |

Thus:

$$\text{SUR} = 6*(n – 2)^2 + 12*(n – 2) + 8$$

$$\text{INT} = n^3 – \text{SUR} = n^3 – 6*(n – 2)^2 – 12*(n – 2) – 8$$

(2) A simpler solution.

The interior is a cube $n – 2$ by $n – 2$ by $n – 2$, and thus:

$$\text{INT} = (n – 2)^3$$

$$\text{SUR} = n^3 – \text{INT} = n^3 – (n-2)^3$$

(3) Slicing.

The top and bottom slices are on the surface.

For each of $n – 2$ middle slices, we have a border of $4*(n – 1)$ cubes.

Thus:

$$SUR = 2*n^2 + 4*(n-1)*(n-2)$$

$$INT = n^3 - 2*n^2 - 4*(n-1)*(n-2)$$

## QUESTIONS

(1) Can you find more formulas?

(2) How do you know that all expressions give the same answer?

  (a) By algebraic transformation of one into another.

  (b) By checking their values for different values of $n$.

  (c) By logic: They are all solutions to the same problem.

(3) Which expressions are the simplest to program?

(4) What percentage of the total volume is INT for different $nv$? (See the following table.)

| $n$ | INT $= (n-2)^3$ for $n > 1$ | total volume $V = n^3$ for $n > 1$ | INT/$V$% $= (n-2)^3/n^3$ |
| --- | --- | --- | --- |
| 1 | 0 | 1 | 0 |
| 2 | 0 | 8 | 0 |
| 3 | 1 | 27 | 3.7% |
| 4 | 8 | 64 | 12.5% |
| 5 | 27 | 125 | 21.6% |
| 12 | 1000 | 1728 | 57.9% |
| 100 | 941,192 | 1,000,000 | 94.1% |
| 1000 | 994,011,992 | 1,000,000,000 | 99.4% |

**LESSON 50   COLORED CUBE**

This unit has been used in classes as low as third grade and as high as eighth grade.

If you connect four of the eight vertices of a cube with diagonals of its faces, the cube's surface is divided into 12 right triangles. In each of the four vertices you connected, six triangles meet. And in the remaining four vertices, three triangles meet.

## ACTIVITY

The task is to color the 12 triangles with three colors such that no two triangles of the same color have a common edge. (Triangles of the same color may only have a common vertex.)

Students are given white poster board or stiff typing paper, rulers, compasses, crayons or markers of three colors, Scotch tape, and scissors. They are told to design a pattern for such a cube, color it, and then cut it out and tape it together with Scotch tape. (The difficulty is in coloring the triangles before you can check how they fit.)

Finally the models are compared to see which ones fulfill the requirements and which are different from each other and in what way.

## SOLUTION

The following figure provides the two different solutions to the problem.

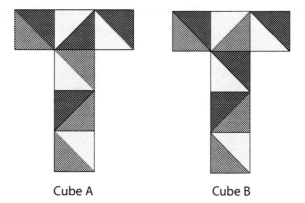

Cube A                    Cube B

*Two different patterns of three colors for the 12 triangles on a cube. When each is folded into a cube, no two triangles of the same color will have a common edge.*

A conceptually difficult question is what it means that two colorings are different. In this lesson we say that two colorings are the same when:

(1) one is obtained from the other by rotating a cube,

(2) one is the mirror image of the other, or

(3) one can be obtained from the other by a permutation of colors, for example, by replacing yellow by blue and blue by yellow.

It is not easy to see whether two cubes are colored the same or differently according to the criteria we have given. The examples on the previous page are the only two different solutions to the problem. Showing that they are different according to the given criteria is not technically difficult, but it is also not easy conceptually.

First you have to make the two cubes according to the patterns given. In each cube, look at the four vertices at which six triangles meet. Observe that cube A has exactly two vertices where each color occurs twice. And cube B has only one such vertex. (See the figure below.)

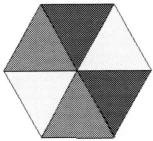
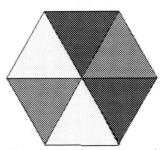

Cube A seen from a vertex in which each color occurs twice.

Cube A seen from a second vertex in which each color occurs twice.

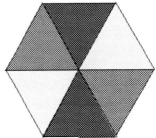

Cube B has only one vertex in which each color occurs twice.

Do not be surprised if some students do not understand the logic of the argument and do not see that this fact, which is easy to observe, actually proves that the two cubes are colored differently according to the criteria.

Showing that these two solutions are the only ones is technically more difficult and should not be attempted, because showing that two solutions are the same can be too difficult for students.

# CHAPTER 4

# Games, Puzzles, and Combinatorics

## LESSON 51   THE FOX AND THE RABBIT

In this board game, a fox tries to catch a rabbit. Children as young as first grade have played it. Children in middle elementary school can make their own boards.

### SUPPLIES

One 4 inch by 6 inch index card; ruler, pencil

### MAKING THE BOARD

On the card, draw a 3 inch by 3 inch square with edges parallel to the card's edges, but draw a diagonal line across a square inch in one of the square's corners. (See the figure below.) Draw lines at 1-inch intervals horizontally and vertically across the square. Make dots at the intersection points, 15 in all. Label one dot "Rabbit" and one "Fox," exactly as shown in the figure.

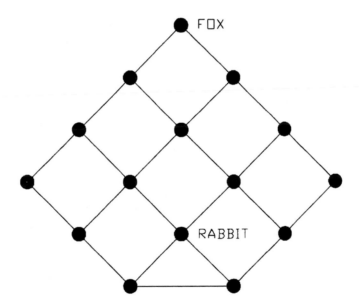

*The board for the fox and rabbit game, with the fox and rabbit at their initial positions*

## PLAYING THE GAME

There are two pieces, one for each player, a fox, FOX, and a rabbit, RABBIT. (We have used a nickel for the fox and a penny for the rabbit. Red and yellow colored markers work as well.)

The fox and the rabbit stand on the locations marked by the dots where their names are written, and they move only along the lines, from dot to dot.

The initial positions are marked in the figure on the previous page. Players take turns. They are not allowed to stand still; they must move. The fox moves first.

The goal of the fox is to capture the rabbit. In order to do so, the fox has to move into the position where the rabbit is standing. It doesn't seem possible, but a smart fox can catch the rabbit.

## SOLUTION

Mark the places on the board with As and Bs as shown in figure 4.2. The fox and the rabbit both start at A. When the fox moves, it moves to B and therefore cannot catch the rabbit. Then the rabbit moves to B, and they are both on the same letter. Now the fox moves back to A, so it cannot catch the rabbit. So the rabbit moves to A, and the whole process is repeated.

The only way for the fox to have a chance to catch the rabbit is if the fox (or the rabbit, if it is stupid!) moves from B to B. So the strategy for the fox is: Walk straight to the bottom of the board, move from B to B, and then start chasing the rabbit! Try it!

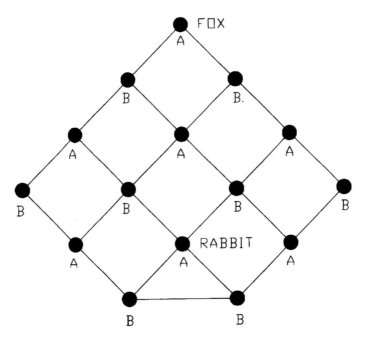

*The board with positions marked with As and Bs.*
*The fox must move from B to B to catch the rabbit!*

## LESSON 52    EARLY ARITHMETIC: FAIR SHARING

Children work in pairs. Each pair gets a set of six small index cards with the numbers 1, 3, 5, 7, 9, and 11.

## TASK

The task is to divide the cards into two (or three) piles in such a way that the sum of the numbers in each pile is the same.  (It is not possible to divide the cards into four or more piles!)

1

3

5

7

9

11

*The six cards needed for the fair sharing task.*

## LESSON 53    FAIR SHARING II

Children work in groups of three. You may need to form one or two groups of two.

### MATERIALS

Prepare for each group a set of nine cards (half of a 3- by 5-inch index card works well). Each card has clearly written on it one 2-digit number. The nine numbers are 19, 27, 37, 46, 55, 65, 73, 81, and 92. Each child should have a calculator.

### TASK

If you are in a group of three, divide the cards among yourselves so that each person has cards whose sum is the same. If you are in a group of two, divide the cards into three piles; the third pile has no owner. (The sum of the values in each of the three piles must be the same, but the number of cards may vary.)

### REMARK

This activity can be taught as a "problem-solving task" in which children solve the problem by any means, and then they discuss how they did it. It can also be taught as a teacher-guided unit on the efficient use of arithmetic.

The two solutions are:

(19, 65, 81) (27, 46, 92) (37, 55, 73)

(19, 65, 81) (27, 37, 46, 55) (73, 92)

### FINDING SOLUTIONS

- Add all numbers; their sum is 495, and thus each child's share must be 495/3 = 165.

- The two biggest numbers, 81 and 92, must be distributed between two different children, because 165 < 81 + 92.

- Now the child who is assigned the number 92 has to find which of the remaining seven numbers (19, 27, 37, 46, 55, 65, and 73) when added to 92 will give a total of 165. The child who is assigned 81 also has to find which of the remaining numbers, when added to 81, will give a total of 165. And the third child just makes suggestions.

## EXAMPLE

A child has 81 to work with,

*   The remaining two numbers must sum to 165 − 81 = 84.

*   The bigger of them is

|     |              |                          |
| --- | ------------ | ------------------------ |
| 65: | 84 − 65 = 19 | My solution is 19, 65, 81. |
| 55: | 84 − 55 = 29 | Not on the list.         |
| 46: | 84 − 46 = 38 | Not on the list.         |

No more solutions that contain the number 81 are possible. Do you see why? Do you see why there are no three numbers that sum to 81?

## REMARK.

In a group of two, one child takes 92, the other takes 81, and the third pile has no owner.

## LESSON 54   BASKETBALL CHAMPS

Children in early grades learn mathematics in a concrete and empirical way, and they learn how to use mathematics in concrete situations. Learning how to reason in the abstract comes later. This lesson shows some simple and elegant reasoning. (This reasoning was attributed to Paul Halmos by Jerry P. King. See King's book, *The Art of Mathematics*, published by Fawcett Columbine, New York, page 183.) The problem given here can be solved by very young children, but understanding the final reasoning happens to be difficult, even for some adults.

### THE STORY

In a school district, 11 schools had basketball teams. They arranged an end-of-season tournament in which, if you lose one game, you are out. How many games were played?

### A SOLUTION

Children may use manipulatives, and work alone or in groups to solve this problem. For an example of solutions, we use pennies ( ○ ). We have 11 teams.

○○○○○○○○○○○

In the first round 5 games are played, and one team waits.

○○  ○○  ○○  ○○  ○○  ○

Five winners and the waiting team are in the second round. So 3 games are played.

○○  ○○  ○○

Three winners are left, so only 1 game is played and one team waits.

○○  ○

Finally the championship game is played (1 game).

○○

Now the total: 5 + 3 + 1 + 1 = 10 games were played.

### OTHER EXAMPLES AND A GENERALIZATION

How many games would be played if the number of teams were different? A table is drawn on a blackboard:

| Number of teams: | Number of games: |
| --- | --- |
| 11 | 10 |

The children, working in groups or individually, provide solutions for different numbers of teams. For example:

| Number of teams: | Number of games: |
|---|---|
| 11 | 10 |
| 8 | 7 |
| 4 | 3 |
| 16 | 15 |
| 7 | 6 |

Do we see a pattern? Yes, the number of games is 1 less than the number of teams. Is this always the case? Of course we can check more cases, but how do we know that we won't find any exceptions?

## A PROOF

We can prove that the number of games is always one less than the number of teams. What does it mean "to prove"? It means to show by some reasoning that it always must be so.

Here is a proof: In each game, one team loses. So the total number of games is the total number of losses. But each team loses exactly once (and is out), except the champion team, who wins all its games.

So the number of games is the number of teams less 1 (less the champs).

## REMARKS

One difficulty in understanding this proof is the part about counting losses. (Why not wins?) To make it more concrete the following sentences may be added to the story:

The organizers prepared consolation prizes. Each losing team was given a basketball. Now the reasoning goes as follows:

- The number of games is the same as the number of basketballs that were given away, because in each game one basketball was given to a losing team.

- Every team except the champion team got exactly one basketball, because the team was out after its first loss.

- So the number of games is the same as the number of basketballs, which is the same as the number of teams less one team (the champion team, who did not lose any games).

## LESSON 55    SUM OF THE FIRST *N* WHOLE NUMBERS

A story about the German mathematician Karl Friedrich Gauss (1777–1855) diring his school years goes like this: The teacher wanted to keep the class busy, so he told students to add up the whole numbers from 1 to 100. But after a few minutes young Gauss presented the following answer:

$$
\begin{array}{c}
1 + \quad 2 + \quad 3 + \ldots + \quad 49 + \quad 50 \\
+ \ 100 + \quad 99 + \quad 98 + \ldots + \quad 52 + \quad 51 \\
\hline
101 + 101 + 101 + \ldots + 101 + 101 = 50{*}101 = 5050.
\end{array}
$$

A general formula, which is true for both even and odd numbers, $n$, is:

$$1 + 2 + 3 + \ldots + n{-}1 + n = n{*}(n + 1)/2.$$

This method is more than just a clever trick. It is used in many problems involving sums. You try to rearrange the computation of a sum so that many additions can be replaced by one multiplication.

As an example, consider this problem:

Add all the odd whole numbers from 1 to 99.

Again, rearrange the computation as previously:

$$
\begin{array}{c}
1 + \quad 3 + \quad 5 + \ldots + \quad 47 + \quad 49 \\
+ \ \ 99 + \quad 97 + \quad 95 + \ldots + \quad 53 + \quad 51 \\
\hline
100 + 100 + 100 + \ldots + 100 + 100 = 25{*}100 = 2500 = 50^2.
\end{array}
$$

A general formula is:

$$1 + 3 + 5 + \ldots + (2{*}n - 3) + (2{*}n - 1) = n^2$$

This technique can be used for computing the sum of the consecutive terms of any arithmetic progression. (An arithmetic progression is a sequence of numbers such that the difference of two consecutive terms is constant.)

If $a_1, a_2, \ldots, a_n$, is any arithmetic progression, then

$$a_1 + a_2 + \ldots + a_n = n{*}(a_1 + a_n)/2.$$

Here, the numbers $a_1, \ldots, a_n$, and their differences do not have to be whole numbers, or even positive numbers.

## LESSON 56   MISSING WORD

The number of three-letter combinations formed from the four letters A, C, T, and G is 64. (Why 64?)

Some of them, such as ACT and CAT, are meaningful English words, but most of them are not. The table below provides the whole list, with just one word omitted.

## TASK

Find the missing word.

| | | | | | | | |
|-----|-----|-----|-----|-----|-----|-----|-----|
| ACT | GTT | CTT | AAC | TCA | CTA | TTA | CAC |
| TGG | GCT | TAC | GGT | AGC | AGT | CTG | ATT |
| TCC | ATG | CGG | TCG | GGG | ACA | CAA | TTC |
| ATA | GTG | CGA | CGC | AAG | CTC | CCG | AGA |
| TCT | GAA | TAT | GCC | CGT | —   | GCA | GTC |
| ACG | GTA | TTT | GAC | CAG | CAT | TGA | CCT |
| TAA | TAG | ATC | CCA | GGA | TGT | TTG | GGC |
| AAT | CCC | GAT | ACC | GCG | AGG | GAG | AAA |

Let children present their solutions before discussing the solution given here.

## SOLUTION

An efficient method for finding the missing word uses the following steps.

(1) Count how many words start with each letter.

Number of words in column:

| First letter: | 1 | 2 | 3 | 4 | 5 | 6 | 7 | 8 | Total: |
|---------------|---|---|---|---|---|---|---|---|--------|
| A | 4 | 1 | 1 | 2 | 2 | 3 | 0 | 3 | 16 |
| C | 0 | 1 | 3 | 2 | 2 | 3 | 3 | 2 | 16 |
| G | 0 | 5 | 1 | 3 | 3 | 0 | 2 | 2 | 16 |
| T | 4 | 1 | 3 | 1 | 1 | 1 | 3 | 1 | 15 |

So we know that the missing word starts with T.

(2) Now look only at the words that start with T, and count how many of them have A, C, G, or T as the second letter.

| TGG | TAG | TAC | TCG | TCA | TGT | TTA | TTC |
|-----|-----|-----|-----|-----|-----|-----|-----|
| TCC |     | TAT |     |     |     | TGA |     |
| TCT |     | TTT |     |     |     | TTG |     |
| TAA |     |     |     |     |     |     |     |

| Second letter: | Number of words: |
|:--------------:|:----------------:|
| A | 4 |
| C | 4 |
| G | 3 |
| T | 4 |

So the second letter of the missing word is G.

(3) Three words start with TG: TGG, TGT, and TGA. Therefore the word TGC is missing!

## DISCUSSION

Discuss how this method could be used if more than one word is missing, when words have different lengths (4, 5, . . . letters), or when more or fewer than four letters are used.

## LESSON 57   THE GAME OF PIG

This game is played as follows.

- You make a "run" by rolling one die as long as you want, providing that you do *not* roll a 1.

- On each roll you score the number of points shown on the die.

- But if you roll one, you lose everything that you gained so far in this run, and the run ends.

Players take turns, and at the end they are ordered depending on their total score. Depending on the number of players, the game may consist of 3-20 runs for each player.

Of course the central question is when to roll again, and when to quit a run and not risk losing what you already have. We are going to look for the "best" strategy, assuming that you ignore other players and simply want to get the best possible average over many games. This assumption is not very realistic. Players usually care more about the game at hand, and therefore they play very conservatively when they are ahead in order to protect their lead, and they take chances when they are behind.

The main difficulty in analyzing games lies not in arithmetic, but in logic. From the "right" point of view, everything becomes clear. But if you take a "wrong" point of view, one difficulty starts piling up on the top of another.

### COMMENT

Let students propose their solutions first. Playing a few runs will make them more familiar with the game.

### A SOLUTION

Look at just one decision at a time. If you quit, you lose nothing and gain nothing. If you decide to roll, you may gain, but also you may lose what you already have. So let's compare expected gains (positive) to losses (negative).

If you have already gained $X$ points in this run, what may happen?

| Outcome on die: | Its probability: | Gain (or loss): |
|:---:|:---:|:---:|
| 1 | 1/6 | $-X$ |
| 2 | 1/6 | 2 |
| 3 | 1/6 | 3 |
| 4 | 1/6 | 4 |
| 5 | 1/6 | 5 |
| 6 | 1/6 | 6 |

Thus the expected gain is:

$$(2 + 3 + 4 + 5 + 6 - X)/6 = (20 - X)/6$$

Therefore if $20 > X$, the expected gain is positive, and you should roll the die. In the long run you would gain. If $20 < X$, the expected gain is negative, so you should quit the run, because you expect to lose. Finally, if $20 = X$, both choices are equally good or bad.

Of course all this reasoning is valid only if the die is fair. Even a small bias may change averages over many trials. The "best" strategy provides an expected gain per run of 8.14180 points.

The six strategies discussed in the book by Bassarear (Bassarear, T. (1997). *Mathematics for Elementary School Teachers*, Boston, MA: Houghton-Mifflin), "stop after $n$ moves" for $n$ from 3 to 8 provide the following expected gains:

| $n$ = number of rolls | Expected gain |
|---|---|
| $n$ = 3 | 6.94444 |
| $n$ = 4 | 7.71605 |
| $n$ = 5 | 8.03755 |
| $n$ = 6 | 8.03755 |
| $n$ = 7 | 7.81429 |
| $n$ = 8 | 7.44218 |

Thus stopping after the fifth and sixth moves provides 98.7 percent of the value for the optimal strategy, making them practically optimal.

Example of a series of 12 runs:

| | | Points |
|---|---|---|
| (1) | 3, 4, 1 | 0 |
| (2) | 2, 2, 6, 1 | 0 |
| (3) | 2, 5, 5, 5, 5 | 22 |
| (4) | 4, 6, 1 | 0 |
| (5) | 4, 3, 1 | 0 |
| (6) | 6, 1 | 0 |
| (7) | 5, 3, 4, 6, 6, 6 | 30 |
| (8) | 2, 4, 6, 3, 1 | 0 |
| (9) | 2, 3, 3, 3, 3, 1 | 0 |
| (10) | 3, 2, 1 | 0 |
| (11) | 4, 3, 3, 6, 4, 6 | 26 |
| (12) | 4, 4, 5, 5, 1 | 0 |
| | sum | 78 |

The average score is $78/12 = 6.5$.

## LESSON 58   PASCAL'S TRIANGLE: AN INTRODUCTION

### TASK 1

Make a rather large square grid with blue horizontal lines (shown as dashed lines in the table below) and red vertical lines (shown as solid lines). Leave a wide margin at the top and on the left side. Number the rows and columns 0, 1, 2, . . . .

### REMARK

In this unit all counting will start with ZERO.

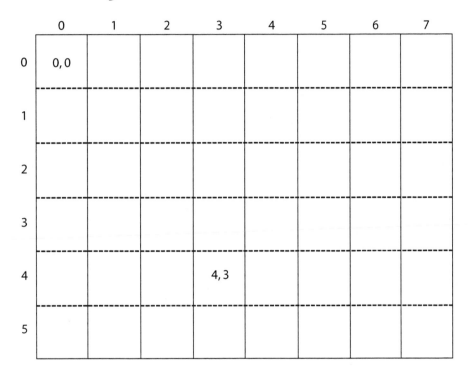

The numbers outside are for quick reference. Square 0, 0 is at the top left corner, square 4, 3 is in the fourth row and third column. Practice naming squares for a while.

### TASK 2

Take a penny or other small token to move on the board you have made. The rules are:

- You always start at square 0, 0.

- You can move your token one square down (a blue move) or one square to the right (a red move).

Answer the following questions:

**Question 1:** How many moves do you need to get to square $i, j$?

**Question 2:** How many blue moves (called $i$) and how many red moves (called $j$) do you need to get to square $i, j$?

**Question 3:** In how many ways can you get to each square $i, j$ on your board? Write this number in its square.

## ANSWERS

(1) It always takes $i + j$ moves to get to square $i, j$.

This number does not depend on the path you choose.

(2) You make $i$ blue moves and $j$ red moves. It doesn't depend on the path you choose.

(3) This question is more complex. But all these values can be computed fast if you observe just three things:

(a) You can get to any square in the top row, $0, j$, in one way (go right, make $j$ red moves).

(b) You can get to any square in the leftmost column, $i, 0$, in only one way (go down, make $i$ blue moves).

(c) If you know the values in the square above, $A$, and in the square to the left, $B$, their sum $B + A$ gives you the value for your square, because each path to it enters either from the left or from above.

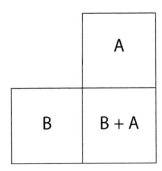

Thus the board will look as follows:

*Table A*

|   | 0 | 1 | 2 | 3 | 4 | 5 | 6 | 7 |
|---|---|---|---|---|---|---|---|---|
| 0 | 1 | 1 | 1 | 1 | 1 | 1 | 1 | 1 |
| 1 | 1 | 2 | 3 | 4 | 5 | 6 | 7 | 8 |
| 2 | 1 | 3 | 6 | 10 | 15 | 21 | 28 | 36 |
| 3 | 1 | 4 | 10 | 20 | 35 | 56 | 84 | 120 |
| 4 | 1 | 5 | 15 | 35 | 70 | 126 | 210 | 330 |
| 5 | 1 | 6 | 21 | 56 | 126 | 252 | 462 | 792 |

## PASCAL'S TRIANGLE

Traditionally this table is rotated to the right 45 degrees and presented as a triangle. The numbers are referred to by their row number, $n = i + j$, and their position in the row, $r = j$. (Remember, counting starts at ZERO!)

```
Row:
0                     1
1                 1       1
2             1       2       1
3         1       3       3       1
4     1       4       6       4       1
5  1      5      10      10       5       1
...    ......................................................
```

Practice finding numbers in the *n*th row at position *r*.

The number in the *n*th row at position *r* is often written C(*n*, *r*) and called a binomial co-efficient. The more traditional notation is:

$$\binom{n}{r}$$

(it looks like a fraction without a bar but in parentheses).

C($n$, $r$) is read "$n$ choose $r$." Thus, for example, 5 choose 2 is 10. The reason for this reading is simple. To get to the $n$th row of Pascal's triangle on your board, you have to make $n = i + j$ moves.

The number of red moves, $r = j$, determines the position in the row. You may choose when to make your red moves. The value in the square gives you the number of paths, namely, the number of ways you may choose $r$ red moves among $n$ moves.

So, for example, consider the square 4, 3. Here, $i = 4$, $j = 3$, and $n = 7$. Looking at Table A, there are 35 ways to arrive at square 4, 3. In all cases, you will make exactly 3 red moves. Here are some possibilities:

> $r\ r\ r\ b\ b\ b\ b$
> $r\ r\ b\ r\ b\ b\ b$
> $b\ b\ b\ b\ r\ r\ r$

Thus C($n$, $r$) is the number of ways you may choose $r$ "things" from a set of $n$ different "things."

On the TI-30X IIS, C($n$, $r$) is computed by [$n$][PRB][→][ENTER][$r$][ENTER].
For example, 12 $n$Cr 7 [ENTER] returns 792.

## PROPERTIES OF PASCAL'S TRIANGLE

At this point do not try to prove anything, but just make observations such as:

- C($n$, 1) = $n$

- C($n$, 2) = $n*(n - 1)/2$, (the "handshake" problem).

- The sum of all elements of one row is a power of two.

- If a row number $n$ is prime, all its elements except C($n$, 0) and C($n$, $n$) are divisible by $n$.

Can you find the Fibonacci numbers, 1, 1, 2, 3, 5, 8, 13, 21, 34, . . . , in Pascal's triangle? Just add the numbers on the lines in the figure below!

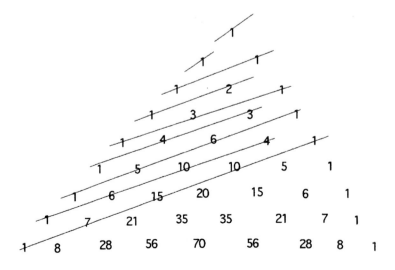

*Sum the numbers on each of the lines,*

## LESSON 59 PASCAL'S TRIANGLE IN EARLY GRADES

Even students in the first grade can be shown how to construct Pascal's triangle. But such an activity doesn't serve much purpose because students at this level do not have enough knowledge to understand its application or use it to solve problems.

However, one valid and challenging task can be done at this level. After the way of constructing a triangle is explained, students are asked to fill in as big a part of it as possible, doing addition solely in their heads. No calculators, paper and pencil computations, manipulatives, or abacus are allowed! Students work individually, not in groups. Writing neatly and aligning the numbers properly should be encouraged.

For this purpose an "array" orientation of Pascal's triangle is preferable.

The first row contains only 1s. You start each other row with 1, and the next number is the sum of the number to the left and the number above.

In this orientation the actual rows of Pascal's triangle look slanted, but the students will not use them. This lesson is only a challenging practice of skills.

EXAMPLE

| 1 | 1 | 1 | 1 | 1 | 1 | 1 | 1 | 1 | 1 |
|---|---|---|---|---|---|---|---|---|---|
| 1 | 2 | 3 | 4 | 5 | 6 | 7 | 8 | 9 | 10 |
| 1 | 3 | 6 | 10 | 15 | 21 | 28 | 36 | 45 | 55 |
| 1 | 4 | 10 | 20 | 35 | 56 | 84 | 120 | | |
| 1 | 5 | 15 | 35 | 70 | 126 | | | | |
| 1 | 6 | 21 | 56 | 126 | 252 | | | | |
| 1 | 7 | 28 | 84 | 210 | | | | | |
| 1 | 8 | 36 | 120 | 320 | | | | | |
| 1 | 9 | 45 | 165 | | | | | | |
| 1 | 10 | 55 | 220 | | | | | | |

As you see, the difficulty of the problem increases quickly.

## LESSON 60   PASCAL'S TRIANGLE: *N* CHOOSE *R*

Calculator: TI-30X IIS

When we count the rows of Pascal's triangle, we always start counting at 0. Similarly, we always start with 0 when we count the numbers in one row of Pascal's triangle.

| Number: | 0 | 1 | 2 | 3 | 4 | 5 |
|---------|---|---|----|----|---|---|
| 5th row: | 1 | 5 | 10 | 10 | 5 | 1 |

Thus the first number of the fifth row is 5, the third number is 10, and the number 1 has positions 0 and 5 in this row. Notice that it doesn't matter if we count backwards instead of forwards; the answers are the same.

If you press the keys [*n*][PRB][→][*r*][ENTER] (*nCr* is read, "*n* choose *r*"), we see on the display the value of the *r*th number from the *n*th row of Pascal's triangle. The numbers *n* and *r* must be whole numbers, and *r* must be smaller than or equal to *n*. The result is a whole number, but if *n* and *r* are big, then only its approximation in scientific notation is shown.

### EXAMPLE

| *n*: | *r*: | *n* choose *r*: |
|------|------|-----------------|
| 5    | 0    | 1 |
| 5    | 2    | 2 |
| 5    | 4    | 5 |
| 5    | 5    | 1 |
| 100  | 50   | 1.008913445e29, which is approximately $10^{29}$ |

Notice that you had to wait quite a while for the answer!

### AN APPLICATION

If we toss a biased coin having a probability of showing heads $h = .6$, and a probability of showing tails $t = .4$, exactly 100 times, then what is the probability that heads will show up exactly 60 times?

It is the fortieth number (which is the same as the sixtieth number!) in the one hundredth row of Pascal's triangle, times $0.6^{60}$ times $0.4^{40}$.

Press:
[.6][^][60][*][.4][^][40][*][100][PRB][→][ENTER][40][ENTER],
and wait. The answer is 0.081219145, which is approximately 8 percent. Thus, the "expected value," 60 heads in 100 tosses, occurs in only 8 percent of situations.

Why do we say "*n* choose *r*"?

Let $n = 5$.

- In how many ways can we choose one element out of a set of five elements? Of course, 5.

- In how many ways can we choose two elements out of five elements? This is the "handshake problem" for five people. The answer is 10 (12, 13, 14, 15, 23, 24, 25, 34, 35, 45).

- Choosing three out of five is just the same as leaving two out, so the number is again 10.

- Similarly choosing four is just leaving one out, so the number is five.

- Finally, choosing five out of five, and choosing 0 (none) out of five can be done in only one way.

Thus we have the numbers from the fifth row of Pascal's triangle.

Is this a general principle? Yes. For example, let 9C4 (= 126) be the number of ways we can choose $r = 4$ elements out of $n = 9$ elements. (Check it with a calculator.) Let's mark one element and leave eight unmarked.

Choosing four elements out of nine can be done in two ways.

(1) Choose the marked element, and choose three out of eight unmarked elements, which can be done in 8C3 (= 56) ways.

(2) Choose four out of eight unmarked elements, which can be done in 8C4 (= 70) ways. Thus, 9C4 = 8C3 + 8C4, which is exactly the rule for building Pascal's triangle row by row: "Add the two numbers above to get a new number below."

| 8th row: | ... | 56 | 70 | ... |
| 9th row: | | ... | 126 | ... |

## REMARK

The elements of Pascal's triangle are also called "binomial coefficients" (see Lesson 61). Algebraic expressions such as $a + b$ used to be called binomials (binomial means "two terms"). The numbers from Pascal's triangle are coefficients in formulas for powers of binomials, so they were called binomial coefficients.

## HISTORY

Pascal's triangle is named after the French philosopher and mathematician Blaise Pascal (1623–1663). But it was already known to Hindu, Chinese, and Arab mathematicians in the eleventh century A.D. In *The Nine Chapters on the Mathematical Art* (p. 226), we find: "In the middle of the eleventh century Jia Xian studied the table of binomial coefficients up to $n = 6$."

## REFERENCE

Kangshen, S., Crossley, J., & Lun, A. W.-C. (1999). *The Nine Chapters on the Mathematical Art*, Oxford: Oxford University Press.

## LESSON 61  PASCAL'S TRIANGLE: BINOMIAL COEFFICIENTS

$(a + b)^2 = (a + b)*(a + b) = a*a + b*a + a*b + b*b = a^2 + 2*a*b + b^2$

$(a + b)^3 = (a + b)^2*(a + b) = (a^2 + 2*a*b + b^2)*( a + b)$

$\qquad = a^2*a + 2*a*b*a + b^2 *a + a^2*b + 2*a*b*b + b^2*b$

$\qquad = a^3 + 3*a^2*b + 3*a*b^2 + b^3$

Can you compute $(a + b)^4$?

Is there an easier way to do it?

An easy way of computing $(a + b)^n$ for different whole numbers $n$ ($n$ can be very large) is provided by Pascal's triangle.

```
Row:
0                               1
1                           1       1
2                       1       2       1
3                   1       3       3       1
4               1       4       6       4       1
5           1       5      10      10       5       1
6       1       6      15      20      15       6       1
...     ................................................
```

The next row always starts with 1 and ends with 1. Besides that, each number is the sum of the two numbers above it.

Notice that the row numbers start with zero. Row number $n$ provides the coefficients for the expansion of $(a + b)n$. So:

$(a + b)^6 = a^6 + 6*a^5*b + 15*a^4*b^2 + 20*a^3*b^3 + 15*a^2*b^4 + 6*a*b^5 + b^6$

The way the next row is created follows from the properties of the multiplication of algebraic expressions. Let's look at the case of constructing the fourth row from the third:

$(a + b)^4 = (a + b)^3*(a + b)$

Thus let's compute $(a^3 + 3*a^2*b + 3*a*b^2 + b^3)*(a + b)$:

$$
\begin{array}{r}
a^3 + 3*a^2*b + 3*a*b^2 + b^3 \\
*\qquad\qquad\qquad a + b \\
\hline
a^3*b + 3*a^2*b^2 + 3*a*b^3 + b^4 \\
a^4 + 3*a^3*b + 3*a^2*b^2 + a*b^3 \\
\hline
a^4 + 4*a^3*b + 6*a^2*b^2 + 4*a*b^3 + b^4
\end{array}
$$

See how the coefficients of the fourth row of Pascal's triangle are the sum of the coefficients of the third row that occur above them.

Pascal's triangle has many applications in algebra, probability theory, and calculus.

## REMARK

If we sum the numbers in one row of Pascal's triangle we get a power of 2.

| Row number: | 0 | 1 | 2 | 3 | 4 | 5 | 6 |
|---|---|---|---|---|---|---|---|
| Its sum: | 1 | 2 | 4 | 8 | 16 | 32 | 64 |

Why is this so? Here is an example for $n = 6$:

$$2^6 = (1 + 1)^6 = 1 + 6 + 15 + 20 + 15 + 6 + 1 = 64$$

## LESSON 62   SQUARE QUILTS

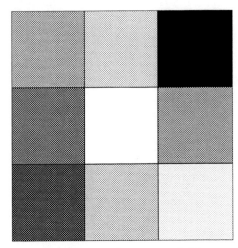

*A square quilt made from nine squares of different colors.*

## MINIMAL PREREQUISITES

- Students should know how to use the TI-30X IIS, or another scientific calculator.

- They should know that n! ([PRB][→][→][ENTER] on the TI-30X IIS) is the number of different ways n things can be listed in order. It is read "n factorial."

- They should know that "n choose r" ([PRB][→][ENTER] on the TI-30X IIS) is the number of ways r elements can be chosen from a set of n different elements.

## RELATED TOPICS

- Formulas for $n!$,

    $n! = 1*2* \ldots *n$ for $n \geq 1$, and $0! = 1$

    (recursive definition) $0! = 1$, and $n! = (n - 1)!* \, n$

- Formulas for binomial coefficients $C(n, r) = nCr$

    $C(n, r) = n!/[r!*(n - r)!]$

- Pascal's triangle

These topics can be taught either before or after this unit.

## MATERIALS

Square sheets from a memo pad in 11 different colors (11 cards per student), Scotch tape

## TASK

You get 11 squares, all of a different color. Choose 9 of them and form a square, a 3 × 3 quilt. Fasten it together with Scotch tape (see the figure above). Use the tape sparingly because your quilt will be viewed from both sides. Sign your name somewhere on it, but with very small letters.

## Question 1

Are all the quilts we made different, or are some the same?

(1) How may we check to see whether two quilts are the same?

Each quilt may be viewed in eight different ways, four from one side and four from the other.

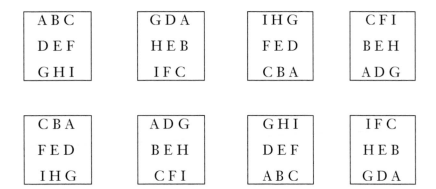

So we must check that two quilts are not just copies of each other that are viewed differently.

(2) Comparing every pair of quilts is a lot of work, so let's classify them into 11 groups by the color in their center (the quilt above would be in category E). We need to compare only quilts belonging to the same category with each other.

(3) Display all the quilts on the blackboard, on a wall, or on a window.

## Question 2

How many different quilts can be made in this way?

- We can choose colors in (11 choose 9) ways.

- We put them row by row (as A B C D E F G H I in the table above) in 9! ways.

- These two things together can be done in (11 choose 9) * 9! ways.

- But each quilt can be put together in eight different ways (see table 4.6).

- Thus the number of quilts is (11 choose 9) * 9! / 8.

Program:

[11] [PRB][→][ENTER][9][*][9][PRB][→][→][ENTER][/][8][ENTER]

Returns:

2494800.

Answer:

2 million 494 thousand 8 hundred.

Can we simplify our program?

Yes, *n*P*r* computes (*n* choose *r*)**r*!, so we can use a simpler program.

Program:

[11][PRB][ENTER][9][/][8][ENTER]

Returns:

2494800

## Question 3

What about rectangular quilts, for example, 2 × 3, or 2 × 4?

A rectangular quilt that is not a square can be made in only four ways. For example,

```
┌─────┐     ┌─────┐
│ A B C│     │ F E D│
│ D E F│     │ C B A│
└─────┘     └─────┘
┌─────┐     ┌─────┐
│ C B A│     │ D E F│
│ F E D│     │ A B C│
└─────┘     └─────┘
```

Thus the formula for their number is (*n* choose *r*)**r*!/4.

[11][PRB][ENTER][6][/][4][ENTER]

Returns:

>83,160

The number of 2 × 3 quilts.

>[11][PRB][ENTER][8][/][4][ENTER]

Returns:

>1,663,200

The number of 2 × 4 quilts.

## About the Authors

**Patricia Baggett** received her B.S. and M.A. in mathematics from Tulane University and the University of Washington and her M.A. and Ph.D. in psychology from the University of Colorado. She has held faculty positions in psychology at Florida International University and the University of Denver. She has been research associate in psychology at the University of Colorado, associate professor of education, University of Michigan, and visiting professor of Computer Science, University of Colorado. Since 1995 she has been professor in the Department of Mathematical Sciences at New Mexico State University, specializing in mathematics education. Her main interests are developing mathematics materials and courses for inservice and preservice teachers, and how children and adults learn mathematical concepts.

**Andrzej Ehrenfeucht** received his master's degree in mathematics from the University of Warsaw in 1955 and his Ph.D., also in mathematics, from the Mathematical Institute of the Polish Academy of Sciences, University of Warsaw, in 1961. He has been on the faculty at the University of California at Berkeley (mathematics), Stanford (philosophy), and the University of Southern California (mathematics and computer science). He is currently professor of computer science at the University of Colorado, where he has been since 1971. His main interests are theoretical computer science, mathematical biology, and elementary mathematics. Together with Prof. Baggett, he has patented an educational game called Tic Tac Twice.